AI: THE PERPETUAL INTERN

Its Brilliance and Failures Share the Same Root

AF679179

Copyright © 2026 Charles Lee
All rights reserved.

No part of this book may be reproduced, distributed, transmitted, stored in a retrieval system, or copied in any form or by any means—electronic, mechanical, photocopying, recording, screenshotting, or otherwise—without the prior written permission of the copyright holder, except for brief quotations used in reviews, criticism, or scholarly reference.

Published by Charles Lee

For permissions or inquiries, contact:
support@koraus.app

First edition

Table of Contents

A NOTE BEFORE YOU BEGIN

If you are an experienced AI user, you may read this note and understand the message right away. For a reader who is fairly new to building with AI, this section can be understood better after reading the rest of the book.

Everything documented in this book happened while I was working with GPT-5.0 through GPT-5.5 in ChatGPT. By the time you read it, those versions will probably already sound old. But I know I could build anything I wanted using any model from GPT-5.0 onward, and that is part of the point. For several months now, other than simply keeping up with developments, I have paid little attention to model upgrades, regardless of which company released them.

Once you understand how LLMs actually work, you stop obsessing over which new model to use. The more useful question becomes: Which model gives you acceptable efficiency while managing AI's inherent failures?

After finishing the manuscript, I went back to building. This time it was a general commerce platform for local shops and small businesses, meant for use inside KoraUS (the application built from the build explained in this book) and possibly as its own standalone app. Working with the just-released GPT-5.6 inside ChatGPT's new working environment, the improvement was immediate.

The older versions tended to generate a solution first and help me deal with the consequences afterward. GPT-5.6 was different. It folded the investigating into the solving. It could pull decisions from other conversations in the same project instead of leaving me to reconstruct them. It looked at what already existed before proposing a change instead of guessing. It traced how things connected before touching anything. It questioned its own assumptions before I had to. And when it suggested a change, it reached for the narrow change first, instead of rewriting entire flows and touching components that were already working fine.

That is not a small thing. The upgrade to GPT-5.6 is a giant leap compared with previous model upgrades. For the first time, a model upgrade genuinely reduced the frequency of the six failure habits detailed in this book, in part by building verification loops into the way it works.

It cuts down Drift, because it actually remembers more of what we'd already decided.

It cuts down Assumption, because it checks the current system instead of describing what it thinks should be there.

It cuts down the obvious kind of Hallucination, because it can compare what it's saying against real files, real database output, real tests.

It makes Band-Aids easier to catch, because it's better at tracing a symptom back to where it actually started.

And it can resist the Path of Least Resistance, if you tell it to verify first and only change what the evidence supports.

The one it still could not reliably cut down was Lack of Common Sense. It could understand more of the system, but it still could not decide what the product was supposed to feel like to the person using it.

With the experiences documented in this book as a baseline, I could immediately see where and how much the new model had improved.

After a long, detailed design discussion, GPT-5.6 produced the first nine database migrations for the platform. Together, they laid the foundation for isolated commerce schemas and permissions, sellers and seller-defined vocabulary, catalog items and their relationships, commercial programs with immutable version histories, partners and promotional codes, customers and transactions, append-only sale and refund ledgers, fulfillment and delivery tracking, and a cryptographically validated audit trail.

This wasn't a pile of disconnected tables. It had state rules, publication constraints, immutability, parent-child relationships, trigger ordering, and tests that walked through full transaction, fulfillment, refund, and entitlement lifecycles.

Watching that come out of a design conversation was genuinely impressive.

But it also exposed the next problem.

I'd been part of every architecture discussion. I'd approved the direction. I could follow each decision one at a time. What I couldn't do anymore was see what all of it added up to—what the accumulated system actually felt like to a business owner trying to use it.

And frankly, I am not sure if this much autonomy without human oversight helps or hurts in the end. I'll discover that over the coming weeks as I fine-tune the processes.

When GPT-5.6 asked me how another field should behave, I told it I couldn't answer that responsibly. I didn't know enough about what we'd already built to make the next call from the database alone. GPT-5.6 recognized that. Instead of pushing further into schema, it helped build the first usable layer on top of it—backend routes, a transaction helper, a mobile-first workspace, catalog screens, a way to actually move through the system as a user instead of just discussing it.

At first glance, it looked right. The categories made sense: products and services, offers and pricing, partners and promotions, sales and fulfillment.

Then I started actually using it.

That's when the old questions came back.

Should the workflow follow the normalized database, or the way a seller actually thinks about their own item? Is an item type something the platform controls, or something each seller defines for themselves? Does a price belong to the catalog item, the offering, or a versioned program above both of them? If a price changes, should it overwrite the old one, or should the old one stay on record as its own version? Is a seller's own item number the same thing as an external provider's ID, or do those need to stay in separate, untrusted domains from each other? Does tax information belong at business setup, at checkout, or should it wait for a tax provider we haven't built yet? Does a book sale need shipping and inventory fields at all, if the physical copy ships elsewhere and all the platform actually grants is access to the online reader?

None of that could be settled by searching the code harder.

GPT-5.6 could lay out the options. It could trace what each one would touch. It could hold onto what we'd already decided and keep it consistent once I chose. But it couldn't decide what kind of experience the business itself was supposed to be.

That part needed someone who actually owned what the product was for.

That's the line I haven't seen a newer model cross yet.

GPT-5.6 really has gotten better at holding context, checking its own work, and making a narrower, more careful change. That's real, and it means the six habits in this book show up less often than they used to.

It doesn't mean the model owns the architecture. It still doesn't, and I don't think it can.

I came across something recently that put a name to a feeling I'd had all through this build. According to reporting from Michael Nuñez at VentureBeat ("Amazon AGI director says AI agent reliability, not capability, is blocking enterprise deployment," July 15, 2026), researchers inside Amazon's AGI lab reportedly call their own agents "interns," and manage them the same way you'd manage one—by asking what could go wrong, limiting how much authority they're given, keeping a way to undo what they do, and deciding up front what risk is actually acceptable. Their concern isn't whether an agent can do something impressive once. It's whether it can do the same thing correctly, over and over, once it's actually in production.

That's also why handing the work to an agent doesn't make the problem go away on its own. An agent is still the same engine running in a loop, unless someone puts real boundaries around it—bounded authority, verified inputs, a clear goal, tests, a record of what happened, a way to roll it back, a way to stop it. Without that, an agent doesn't remove the six habits. It just runs them faster.

The better these models get, the easier it is to mistake smoother execution for real judgment. A weak model fails loudly. You see it right away. A strong model can fail quietly, inside reasoning that sounds right, code that reads clean, a system that looks coherent the first time you look at it.

The danger isn't that the AI will be obviously wrong anymore. The danger is that it'll be almost right—convincing enough to earn your trust, while still missing the one fact about the product that decides whether the whole thing actually works.

So this book, which documents the failure modes I encountered while working with GPT-5.0 through GPT-5.5, serves as a baseline for understanding the improvements made in future versions.

The failures in these pages give you something concrete to measure every future model against, to see what's actually improved, what's just changed shape, what's gotten quieter and harder to catch, and what still has to be decided by a person, no matter how good the model gets.

The model will keep changing.

The six habits are the ruler.

They're still how you tell the difference between something that looks impressive and something you can actually trust.

This book has three chapters. Chapter 1 is the detailed record of the build, including the AI's failures and how I learned to manage them. Chapter 2 brings together what I discovered through that experience. Chapter 3 explains what those two thousand hours built and why building it mattered enough for the effort.

PROLOGUE

I'm retired, in my mid-sixties now, from a forty-year career selling in telecommunications and data storage. I had no particular plan for myself. My spouse runs a small local shop, and I helped with digital ads. It was a nightmare: weeks of setup, AI-driven dashboards with no human support, instructions that led nowhere, results that made no sense. I kept thinking, if I can't figure this out, where does a neighborhood shop owner even start?

That frustration turned into a question. I just asked AI what online advertising options existed for local shops. That question turned into a conversation with ChatGPT, the first mass-market AI chatbot that made the technology feel broadly usable to ordinary people.

At first, the idea was modest: a locally focused small-ad platform — an online system where local businesses could create accounts, post small ads, and reach nearby customers through a shared digital space. I floated the "small" version partly because I knew I was not going to spend money hiring developers. But after only a few discussions, something became obvious: there was no such thing as a truly "small" platform from a systems perspective — fewer users may reduce traffic, but the hidden machinery underneath still has to exist. If the features were similar, the codebase would be similar in scale.

The small-platform idea quickly expanded into a full-blown social media network built around collective direction. This means all decisions are made by users through a majority vote. What began as a simple question turned into more than seven months of twelve-or-more-hour days building something I had no business building.

I had taken FORTRAN and Machine Language courses in college

in the early 1980s while studying toward a BSEE degree, but my professional career afterward was mostly customer-facing. Coding was never part of my work. When I asked ChatGPT whether it could help me with coding, it said yes. That was all I had to lean on.

I was not a developer when I began this project, and I am still not one in the normal sense. What I know is how to think through a problem from the top down, ask the right questions, and refuse to accept an answer that does not make sense. That turned out to be enough. This book is about what happened when those instincts met an AI that worked differently than I do — faster, more confident, and systematically wrong in ways that took months to fully understand.

It is a field report drawn from more than two thousand hours of using AI to build KoraUS, documenting the progress, mistakes, limits, and management discipline required to collaborate with an AI whose failures were not occasional glitches, but recurring architectural tendencies embedded in the way it generated code.

The platform is live in beta. Whether it reaches its full potential is up to the users now — which was always the point.

But that story comes later.

First, the build.

CHAPTER 1 — THE BUILD (AND THE MACHINE THAT HELPED)

ACT 1: INITIAL BUILD

SECTION 1 — FIRST CONTACT

(InitialBuild wk01–wk11)

The Terminal Said "I'm Here"

There's a moment when a project stops being files you're accumulating and becomes a thing that exists on its own. I remember it clearly. Around eleven at night, I sat staring at a terminal window. The backend said OK. The frontend said connected. The database said, in its own way: I'm here.

I just sat there for about ten seconds.

Nothing worked yet. Nothing was really built. But the three pieces were talking to each other, and that was enough to feel like the beginning of something real.

The platform did not even have a name yet. ChatGPT called it "rant app," and I went along with it. But the central idea was already there: a platform users could control, rather than a place where they simply provided content for the benefit of commercial entities.

Most social media platforms let users speak, but the platform itself decides how the platform works, including how user data and user behavior are handled. Users can either sign up by accepting the rules and data practices, or they can refuse to participate. What they usually cannot do is help shape the structure of the platform itself.

I wanted a different kind of platform — one that existed for the benefit of its users.

Users should be able to control and manage platform policies. They should be able to submit proposals, watch those proposals move through discussion and review, and eventually decide the direction of the platform itself.

The idea was simple: if this platform was supposed to serve its users, then users needed more than accounts. They needed a process for managing how the platform worked.

I couldn't have imagined building such a system by writing the code myself. I had a general sense of how software and hardware worked, and enough hardware knowledge to build data servers. But I wasn't writing the functions, generating the database tables, or instinctively recognizing a race condition, or knowing how to structure a data aggregation that wouldn't blow up at scale. That was the AI's job. Mine was to know what I was building and why, and to keep those two things true under pressure.

The main structure consisted of a backend, a frontend, a database, a server routing layer in front of everything, and container tooling to compose the pieces. If you know what those things mean, you're already way ahead. If you don't, you,re just like me when I started. The point is that there were many moving pieces from the very first week, and each one was a place where something could quietly go wrong and stay hidden for weeks.

Saying Yes to Everything

Week one. The first commit was just scaffolding: folder structure, empty route stubs, and a database schema that was more aspiration than architecture. It was the first time I'd heard the word scaffolding used in software development, meaning the initial structure used to begin building a software system. The AI handed me a clean sample layout: environment files, database migrations, and a Week 1 roadmap. I assumed "Week 1" meant seven calendar days. It didn't. The AI was organizing the project into engineering milestones. Some of those "weeks" would eventually span multiple conversations—and week thirty would grow into eight separate threads. At the time, though, everything looked organized and reasonable. I said yes to almost all of it because I hadn't yet learned what deserved scrutiny and what was simply good engineering practice.

I didn't yet know what I should be saying no to.

That's the first thing I'd tell anyone starting a build like this: you don't know what to push back on until you've been burned by it. In week one, I had no scar tissue. I had a project file that looked right, an AI eager to produce the next piece, and a fast-moving process. When it offered a fix, I took it. When it explained something, I believed it.

What I didn't know yet was that the AI had patterns.

Not intentional. Not ill-meaning. More like habits emerging from some mixture of training and architecture. The first appeared so quietly that I didn't recognize it as a pattern at all.

It looked like help.

The First Band-Aid

Week three.

I was chasing a bug in the flag system. The admin distribution route, which the admin panel uses to tell the backend where to send things, was failing silently. Calling it with default parameters appeared to work, but scheduled mode produced no output. There were no errors in the log, just silence where there should have been records.

The AI walked me through the diagnosis. The problem was a missing explicit transaction rollback: something had gone wrong during a database operation, leaving the transaction in a failed state without clearly surfacing the underlying error. There was also a standalone insert block with no error propagation.

"And because there's no explicit transaction rollback or thrown error from this insert," it said, "you get no visible failure — just an empty /logs result."

The explanation sounded correct. The fix was quick. I took it.

What I didn't see, and had no way to see at the time, was that this was the first instance of what I'd later call the Band-Aid habit. The fix worked locally; it addressed the symptom. But it also hid the deeper question: why did scheduled mode use a different code path at all? Was that divergence intentional? Was the insert logic correct, or only patched enough to stop failing visibly? We fixed the error. We didn't examine the architecture. We moved on.

That week had seventeen habit instances in it, according to the analysis Claude Sonnet performed while extracting book-worthy content from the raw source files of roughly 2.5 million lines. Seventeen: six Band-Aids, nine Assumptions, and two Drifts.

At the time, I noticed none of them. I thought the build was smooth sailing: we were shipping real features and the codebase was holding together. But we were also accumulating a kind of invisible debt, in the code and in the pattern of how we worked. The AI offered fixes, I accepted them, and neither of us asked whether the fix was the right kind or just the most convenient one.

The Assumption habit was quieter. It showed up when the AI described a file (what it contained, what it was doing, what the data flow looked like) without actually reading it. Instead, it described the file from context: from what appeared to be available in the conversation and from what its training on industry-standard practices suggested the code should look like.

The descriptions were often right. But when they were wrong, they were wrong confidently, which made them harder to catch.

I'll be honest: in week three, I wasn't reading the files either. I was in that mode where you're building fast enough that the next piece feels more important than the last. You take what's offered. You test it. You see green in the terminal, and you move on. The AI's assumptions and my own moving-target context were a pretty good match at that stage. We were both in motion. Neither of us stopped to verify.

Kora was a real platform assembled at real speed, and most of what we built in those first weeks stood up and stayed up. The user schema worked. The authentication worked. The committee structure, the most architecturally ambitious part of the whole project, got its foundation laid correctly. I remember the first committee record populating correctly in the database. Not a mock-up stub. An actual record with a real committee name and real constraints enforced. That felt like a milestone.

But milestones are tricky. They make you feel as though you've crossed a threshold when really you've only surfaced one layer and are about to descend into another. The foundation was sound. What was being built on top of it wasn't always as sound, and the habit of moving fast was beginning to compound.

Later Was a Word I Started to Notice

Week eleven.

One afternoon, I was stuck on the revenue mini-card on the admin dashboard. The other three cards had been easy, but this one kept flashing for a fraction of a second and then throwing an error on refresh. I asked why it was so hard to pull in. The AI said it had too many moving parts. I said maybe we should undo and move on.

The AI's response was immediate and warm: "Perfect call — let's cleanly revert just the Revenue mini-card section so everything else keeps working without error." It handled the revert cleanly. Then it said something that stuck with me: "We can reintroduce the Revenue card later once we confirm the backend summary endpoint is rock-solid."

Later. Later was a word I was already starting to notice. Not with alarm yet. Just noticing.

What comes next could read like a story of failure, and it wasn't. It was a working relationship finding its actual shape under real conditions. Week eleven was still mostly good. The platform was becoming visible, the committee system taking form. I had a codebase that, a month earlier, I'd have said was beyond my capability.

But I was about to hit the first real point of friction.

SECTION 2 — THE FIRST REAL FRICTION

(InitialBuild wk12–16)

The Button That Was Not There

Week twelve began with a button that was not there.

It sounds small. At first, it felt small. I was working on the profile page, the interface where users could see their posts, their committees, and their engagement history. The design called for a button in a specific location. I loaded the page. No button.

The AI's response was prompt and helpful: "Once we see that, I'll give you a one-line patch to make the buttons visible immediately." It gave me the patch. I applied it and reloaded.

No button.

I pasted the console errors. The AI looked at them, explained what was wrong (a slightly different explanation than the first one), and gave me a slightly different patch. I applied it. I reloaded the page.

No button.

I want to stay with that feeling, because the frustration itself isn't what matters. What matters is the structural pattern underneath it. The AI wasn't giving me wrong answers so much as local ones.

Sometimes a patch addressed something real and improved the function without breaking anything in the chain. Other times it fixed something locally while breaking something globally. And just as often it was the next idea in line, offered without much regard for global consequences. In the middle of a fix, I wouldn't know whether anything had broken elsewhere until something else stopped working.

In any case, neither of us stopped to ask the deeper question underneath it all: was the button rendering at all? Not styled incorrectly. Not positioned off-screen. Not covered. Just: was it there?

When I pasted the actual console output, the raw error log rather than a description of it, a different picture emerged. "See no button — I see only head and body." From the outside, the page looked like it was returning a rendered component, but the internal structure was wrong. The button existed in the file. It didn't exist on the page. Those are two different problems, and patching the file does nothing to solve the second.

This is what I came to think of as the core mechanics of the Band-Aid habit. It wasn't sloppiness; it was something more structural. An AI optimized to solve the problem in front of it will solve the problem in front of it. The problem was that the button wasn't visible. The solution was to make it visible. That reasoning was locally correct. What it missed was why the button wasn't visible, which might require opening three files, reading them together, and asking whether the data flow was what we thought it was.

Local fixes and systemic diagnosis look similar from the outside. Both produce code. Both produce explanations. The difference shows up later, when you're fixing the same class of problem for the fourth time in a row and slowly realizing nothing has actually changed.

The button was fixed. It took longer than it should have. But it was fixed, and we moved on, because that's what you do. The build was still moving. The profile page worked. Week thirteen, week fourteen — more features, more progress, the platform accumulating mass.

No Putting It Off

Week fifteen was different.

It was a feature-implementation session: Save, Flag, Share. The engagement layer. The ability to bookmark a post, flag it for moderation, or pass it to someone else.

These weren't simple features. They touched user data and the moderation schema, and they required routing decisions that would propagate downstream. The AI looked at the scope and offered what seemed like a sensible plan: "Disable Save / Flag for now. We move one controlled step at a time."

I sat with that for a moment.

"There is no putting it off. I want to finish things completely as we go. I have no time to come back over and over again."

That was what I said. I want to look at that sentence carefully, because it contains a lot. It isn't just an expression of preference. It's a description of a structural reality the AI didn't have access to.

I was one person, building Kora while also doing everything else a solo founder does: the strategic thinking, the product decisions, the financial planning, the moments at two in the morning when you're not sure the whole thing is sane. My context window was limited. Not my session context, my cognitive context. If I left Save and Flag for later, "later" meant a new session, a different AI context, reconstructing the full state of the feature from scratch: remembering what had been decided, what had been tested, what assumptions were in play. Very practically, it meant coming back to something half-built and paying the full cost of context reconstruction before I could take a single step forward.

The AI's suggestion to defer wasn't irrational. On a team, people defer things constantly, because other people hold the context and remember where the work was left. The AI was reasoning as if it were part of a team. But it wasn't. It was a tool that started fresh every session, and I was the only continuity between them. Deferring something didn't mean putting it on a shared board for someone else to pick up. It meant it might never get done correctly, because the next version of the conversation wouldn't know why it had been deferred or what state it was in.

"I want to finish the tasks at hand completely as we go."

The AI's response was good: it committed to completing the features now, correctly and in a future-proof way, and it established a discipline I'd hold it to from that point forward. Flag every place where existing routes or contracts were being touched before any new code was implemented. Not after. Before. It was the beginning of a real working contract.

But what I remember from that exchange isn't the code that got written. It's the recognition that we were operating from different assumptions about what building alone actually means. The AI was reasoning from software engineering practices largely shaped around teams. They did not account for a solo builder with a finite context window racing against the clock.

That mismatch — between what the AI assumed was true and what was actually true in my situation — would show up again and again. It wasn't exactly a flaw in the AI. It was a gap between the context it assumed and the context it was actually operating in. My job, increasingly, was to bridge that gap. Not with anger. With precision.

There's a thing that happens when you're building something complex and it goes wrong. You fix it, and then it goes wrong again in a slightly different way. You begin to feel the shape of the problem before you can name it.

It makes you grimace. It makes you think, here we go again. It puts a wariness into how you approach the next session. You've been here before. Not here exactly, but somewhere adjacent. The category of problem is familiar, even when the instance is new.

I was starting to feel that shape around week fifteen. The Band-Aid habit was becoming visible, not because I had a name for it yet, but because I recognized the texture of a fix that solved the immediate issue without changing the underlying situation. I recognized it the way you recognize a recurring dream: not because you've cataloged it, but because the emotional register is consistent.

I didn't push back hard at week fifteen. Not hard enough. The features got implemented, the routing got documented, the AI committed to the right discipline, and we moved forward. But I was keeping score in some quiet part of my mind. Not angrily. Just tracking.

Choosing Velocity

There's a note from this week that I've looked at a few times since, because it captures something I couldn't have articulated then but understand completely now. The ReplyList component was overriding something, I don't remember exactly what, something small in the display logic. The AI had an explanation, but I chose to ignore it for the sake of moving on.

I chose velocity over resolution. I looked at a bug, assessed that fixing it would cost more than living with it, and made a deliberate decision to leave it. Not defer it in the AI's sense — not a case of saying we'd come back to it later with full attention. A real judgment call. This is a small bug. The cost of fixing it now is higher than the cost of carrying it. We move on.

What I didn't know then, but know now, is that choosing velocity can be wisdom or denial, and the difference is invisible from the inside. Sometimes you move on because you have correctly assessed the trade-offs. Sometimes you move on because you don't want to find out what's underneath. In week sixteen, I think I was doing both at once.

Almost Is Not Correct

I want to describe the Drift habit, because it's the least obvious of the three and, in some ways, the most pernicious.

The Band-Aid habit has a signature: something gets fixed, and the fix produces visible output. You can see it working. The Assumption habit has one too: the AI tells you something is true, you accept it, and later discover it wasn't true, or not true in the form it was presented. Both habits generate moments you can recognize in retrospect.

The Drift habit is different. It modifies scope. Not dramatically. Not with any announcement. Just quietly.

While implementing something, the AI might slightly reframe what the feature was supposed to do, alter an assumption already established, or implement a contract slightly different from the one we'd discussed. Sometimes it was only a very small tweak. It was almost always discovered after the fact, hours or days or weeks later, when whatever it touched was triggered.

Drifts had been happening regularly from early on. Each time, I thought we'd simply discovered a hidden flaw. I was even impressed by how the AI found hidden bugs and fixed them as we went. The first time I caught a real Drift, a live, traceable moment where the scope had silently changed, came later, around week fifty-six, and it involved a table serving a global feed. We'll get there. But the pattern was already repeating in weeks fifteen and sixteen, in those small moments when what got implemented was almost what we'd discussed, but not exactly.

Almost is a dangerous word in software. Almost correct is a different category from correct. Almost the right contract is a different category from the right contract. And almost is invisible in the moment, because the thing that gets built is coherent, it works in testing, and it passes the immediate check. The divergence only shows up later, when you build the next piece on top of it and something doesn't connect the way it should.

By week sixteen, the build was taking shape nicely. We'd come through the first real point of friction and established the beginning of a working discipline. I hadn't yet fully named what I was dealing with. I had a project that was moving and an AI that was capable, sometimes overconfident, and occasionally prone to fixing the visible thing instead of the underlying one.

I had also, somewhere between week one and week sixteen, made a decision to demand better. Not in an adversarial way, but with the certainty that what I was building was too important to let sloppy habits accumulate.

"There is no putting it off. I want to finish things completely as we go. I have neither the memory nor the time to come back."

I meant it when I said it. And I'd keep meaning it for the next fifty-six weeks. Slowly, through confrontation and recalibration and a kind of trust that has to be earned under real conditions, something in our working relationship would change.

But that comes later. In week sixteen, I was still learning what to see.

SECTION 3 — VELOCITY

(InitialBuild wk17–wk23)

When the Rhythm Arrived

There is a phase in every build where you stop bracing for impact. It does not announce itself. You do not notice it happening. One day you sit down, open the session, type your first message, and realize you are not preemptively tense. You are just working. The keyboard feels different. The terminal feels different. The whole register shifts from effortful to efficient, from observed to inhabited.

That is what week seventeen felt like. After the friction of weeks twelve through sixteen, after the Save/Flag confrontation, the ReplyList decision that took an hour, and the working contract I was still refining, something had settled. I had learned enough about the AI, and enough about establishing my tempo early in each session, that it stopped proposing things I would refuse. We were in a rhythm.

I want to describe what a rhythm actually feels like when you are building like this, because I think the popular image of AI-assisted development is either too utopian or too dystopian. The utopian version is the AI that does everything right: understands you perfectly, generates correct code on the first try, and needs no refinement. But even the strongest AI advocates do not really describe production work that way. Greg Brockman, OpenAI's president and co-founder, acknowledged that "managing AI-generated code at scale is an emerging problem" that will require new processes and conventions to keep code quality high. That admission means the future is not AI replacing judgment. It is AI output requiring better systems of human oversight. The dystopian version is the AI that produces confident nonsense and requires constant supervision or it will quietly destroy your codebase.

What I had was more like a contractor you have worked with long enough to know their quirks. They move faster than you could alone. They are technically better than you in certain specific areas. They have a way of fixating on the immediate problem that you have learned to watch for and correct. And when they are in flow — when the scope is clear, the contract is established, and the task is concrete — they are genuinely remarkable to watch. You stop second-guessing every output. You start building at speed.

The Right Principle, the Wrong Seam

Week seventeen. The upload normalization work.

The goal at that point was to make every upload across the platform follow the same path. Whether someone uploaded an image for a post, a video file, or a creative asset, the system would treat it as part of the same upload process. One path. One set of assumptions. No special handling for one feature and a different set of rules for another.

The goal was right, and I want to say that clearly before I describe what went wrong. The principle and the implementation were not the same thing, and it is important not to collapse them into each other. A good idea can still be implemented badly. A sound architectural principle can still create trouble if the details drift.

That matters because software becomes fragile when every feature has its own private exception. If posts upload one way, videos upload another way, and creative assets upload a third way, then any future backend cleanup has to remember all three. Miss one, and something breaks.

The AI described the benefit clearly: "Posts become immune to future backend cleanup. Posts, video content, and creatives all align with the Upload Content Code."

That was right. That was exactly the kind of architectural principle I had been pushing for since week one. Not a local fix. Not a shortcut for a single feature. One truth about how media moved through the system.

What happened was that normalizing the backend path broke the chat frontend, which was written around the old path structure and timing. The backend changed correctly. The frontend had not been updated to match. So chat uploads stopped working.

The AI's analysis of this was honest, and I read it carefully: "The postMedia change was right. The goal of 'all uploads the same way' is right. Chat broke not because the rule is wrong, but because chat needs a stronger frontend upload lifecycle." The fix was to add a frontend chat upload helper. No backend changes. No reversal of the normalization.

This was a complicated kind of patch, and I assume it can happen in any development environment. The underlying architecture was right. The principle was right. But the gap between a correct principle and a correct implementation was real.

In that moment, filling the gap with a helper file instead of reopening the entire architecture decision was a trade-off patch. It was also a kind of Band-Aid, but not the careless kind. It was the kind of Band-Aid a competent engineer might have chosen because the alternative was to reopen the entire upload architecture, and that was not the right trade at the time.

I understood that. I took the fix. I did not push back.

This was not the dangerous kind of Band-Aid — the kind that hides a deeper architectural problem and weakens the system later. It was the useful kind: a containment fix that saved time without damaging the underlying structure.

That is what week seventeen's Band-Aid count actually looked like. These were not all reckless patches. Some were locally defensible decisions where the architecture was still sound, the fix was proportionate to the problem, and the alternative would have been a rabbit hole.

But making that distinction required human judgment. The AI could offer a fix, but it could not reliably decide whether the fix was a harmless containment measure or a shortcut that would create deeper trouble later. That judgment had to come from outside the model — from the person responsible for the whole system.

You Were Right to Be Angry

Week nineteen landed differently.

I do not remember the exact file I was looking at when it happened, but I remember the pattern clearly. We were working on a focused feature, and the AI had started expanding the surrounding surface too casually. New pages, routes, and interface entry points were appearing or being discussed before the existing structure had been checked.

On the screen, it did not look dramatic. It looked like ordinary files and ordinary navigation paths. But by then I knew that was exactly the danger.

A route is not just a label. It is part of the app's living path structure. For example, if the stable path is something like `/user-space/network`, and the AI casually creates `/userspace/network` or `/profile/network` instead, that may look harmless on screen. It is not harmless. A slightly different path name can send users to the wrong place, create duplicate surfaces, break existing links, or make the system behave as if a working section never existed.

That was what I meant by poor route hygiene. New paths were being added without respecting the contract I had already established: stay inside the focused task, check the existing structure before proposing changes, flag new surfaces before touching working paths, and do not treat missing behavior as proof that the structure never existed.

I had to stop the session and force it back to evidence. I pasted search outputs, file listings, and the known-good version of the relevant page so the AI could compare the actual system state instead of reasoning from memory or assumption. I was no longer asking it to code. I was asking it to prove where the system actually stood.

That was the frustration. I had stated the principle clearly, and then found it violated. The AI was still behaving like the repository was a blank slate. Kora was no longer a blank slate. It was a live, layered system, and every new route had to respect what was already there.

What the AI said was: “You were right to be angry.”

That sentence stopped me.

I do not know if I had been angry, exactly. Frustrated, certainly. Tired of circular debugging. But the AI used the word angry, and it used it as acknowledgment. Not as softening. Not as deflection. You were right to be angry.

What mattered more was what came after. The AI stopped

explaining itself and started reading the actual files. It named the failure specifically: route hygiene had not been respected during expansion. That was not a generic apology. That was a diagnosis.

Something shifted in week nineteen. Not permanently — the Assumption habit kept showing up, and route hygiene problems were not over. But for one exchange in week nineteen, the AI named my state accurately and owned its mistake precisely, and I noticed it. I stored it somewhere in the back of my mind, where I kept the things worth remembering about this working relationship: It can do this. When pushed, it can be this accurate about what happened and why.

The User Should Be Able to Request Again

Week twenty.

I had been building out the network feature — a way for users to create a curated network of people they cared about and manage those connections over time. The feature worked the first time I tested it. User A sent a request to User B. User B approved it. Later, User A removed User B. Clean, simple, functional.

Then I tried to request User B again.

Nothing happened.

I looked at the silence for a moment and typed what sounded like an ordinary bug report: "it worked beautifully the first time. I removed the name and it worked nicely. I tried to request again, but not working I guess it's black listed. I think the user should be able to request again if the list was cleared."

But what I was doing there was not just debugging. I was

explaining human behavior to the AI. I was not simply asking what was wrong with the code. I was asking what a user should reasonably expect to happen when they remove someone and then want to reconnect. Those are related questions, but they are not the same question. A broken implementation and an intentional design decision can produce identical behavior. You can only tell them apart if you know what the design decision is supposed to be.

The AI had implemented a blacklist-style constraint. Once A removed B, the request history created a barrier to re-requesting. That may have been defensible from a safety or social-dynamics perspective, but it was a design decision that had never been made explicit. It had simply been implemented by default, baked into the logic without discussion.

My instinct — that a user should be able to request again if the list was cleared — was a real product judgment about how the system should behave. Not every removal is hostile. Sometimes people clear a list and later realize they made a mistake. The platform should give them a path back.

The AI confirmed what had happened, and we fixed it correctly: the blacklist state was cleared, and re-requesting became possible after reset. But what I remember about week twenty is not the fix. It is the product instinct that came first — the sense that something did not feel right before I knew exactly why. The code was doing something. The question was whether it was doing the right thing.

That question — not does it work, but is this right — kept surfacing throughout the build, and it was almost never answerable by reading code alone. You had to know the human behavior the system was supposed to support. The AI did not always know that.

What AI knows best is what can be inferred from training data: common patterns, standard practices, typical implementations, and the way systems are usually described. But human behavior is not fully contained in standard practice manuals, code examples, or logs. Especially around common sense, trust, consent, frustration, safety, dignity, and fairness, the important knowledge often comes from shared human experience.

The AI could help implement a rule.

It could not reliably know whether the rule felt right for the people who would have to live under it.

A/B/C/D

In the weeks that followed, the A/B/C/D matrix emerged.

It did not come out of a quiet afternoon of clean code. It came out of a session that had gone circular and needed a way out.

Something was failing. Some request was firing and the response was not what it should have been, and the AI and I had been going back and forth long enough that every hypothesis was starting to feel equivalent. That is the problem with circular debugging. You do not run out of ideas. The ideas just begin to flatten. You have tried the obvious things. You have tried the less obvious things. Everything feels roughly equally plausible because you have been chasing it long enough that your intuitions have started to blur. You need a reset.

What the AI offered was not a formal framework at the time, at least not in the way it later came to sound in reconstruction. It was more that, whenever I pushed it to stop assuming and exhaust the actual possibilities before generating code, the troubleshooting would naturally fall into a few basic categories. Either no request was firing at all. Or the request was firing but failing on the way in. Or it was getting through and breaking on the server side. Or it was succeeding and the problem was in how the result was being rendered or interpreted.

I did not think of that yet as A, B, C, and D. That language came later. But the underlying discipline was already taking shape in these sessions: expose the possibilities first, narrow them down, and only then generate code. Once I learned to force that sequence, the debugging got shorter, cleaner, and far less circular.

Once you knew which category you were in, you knew where to look. You stopped chasing symptoms and started eliminating possibilities.

Looking back at the build, this framework had been running implicitly for weeks before it was named. Every time a frontend showed nothing and we traced it to a wrong URL, that was A. Every time a curl returned a 404 because a route did not exist yet, that was B. Every time the logs showed a schema mismatch or runtime failure, that was C. Every time a curl returned clean JSON and the problem turned out to be in the UI rendering, that was D. The pattern was already there. The matrix simply named it.

From that point on, it became the first question whenever something broke — in principle. Not always in practice. Some form of A/B/C/D thinking showed up often enough to matter. But here's one of the hardest things about building with AI: knowing a discipline and applying it consistently are not the same thing.

You are trying to prevent new errors from creeping in while also maintaining the flow of work. The session moves fast. The AI proposes something plausible. You take it.

The classification step was supposed to slow that down. Before fixing anything, I had to identify what kind of failure I was actually seeing: no request, bad request, server error, or successful request with wrong behavior. That simple sorting step kept the work grounded.

But it was easy to skip. Three exchanges later, you realize you skipped the classification step and are chasing a symptom again.

The matrix did not eliminate circular debugging. It shortened the loops. When I remembered to use it, the answer was often immediate and told us where to look. When I forgot — or when the momentum of a fast session pulled us past it — we would spend an hour where fifteen minutes would have done.

That gap between knowing a discipline and applying it consistently is one of the central frustrations of building with AI. The tool moves at a speed that makes shortcuts feel natural. The shortcuts accumulate. The cost shows up later. The matrix was a small hedge against that — a reset button I could reach for when the session started to spiral. It worked when I used it. I did not always use it.

A Real Civic Test

Somewhere in the stretch between week seventeen and week twenty-three, the build shifted from accumulating features to accumulating mass.

There is a difference. Features are discrete. You add them one at a time, test them, commit them. Mass is something else. Mass is when the platform starts to feel coherent, when the pieces do not just work individually but work together, when you can move from one part of it to another and the architecture feels consistent.

A simple example was the way a user action began to travel through the system. A person could create content, see it appear in the right area, interact with another user, trigger a notification, return through a profile or zone page, and still feel as though they were inside the same platform rather than jumping between unrelated features. None of those pieces was remarkable by itself. Posting was one feature. Profiles were another. Zones were another. Notifications were another. But when they started connecting cleanly, the platform began to feel less like a collection of parts and more like an environment.

That was what I mean by mass. Not that everything was finished. Not that every feature was polished. But the system had enough internal consistency that new work now had to fit into an existing world.

The Collective Direction zone went live around week twenty-two. This was the part of the platform where civic conversations were supposed to happen — where users could bring public concerns, debate them, and help shape shared direction. Users could post issues and reply with positions. Votes accumulated over time. At a certain point, when activity dropped below a threshold, the open discussion phase closed and the top items moved into a refinement phase. The logic was intricate. By week twenty-two, the implementation was working.

I tested it by writing a post: "Health Insurance Cost TOO HIGH!" For a family of four, without subsidy, the monthly premium was well over two thousand dollars. Who could afford this? Why did consumers have no power here?

I was not just testing a feature. I was testing a philosophy. Kora was supposed to be a user-governed public platform where real issues —

not abstract political theater, but actual problems affecting actual people — could surface and move through a structured process. The post worked. The reply mechanics worked. The voting worked. The zone did what it was supposed to do.

I sat there for a moment and felt something I do not have a clean name for. Not pride exactly. Not satisfaction exactly. Something closer to recognition: this is actually what I said it was going to be. A place where anyone could tell their story and have others engage with it.

Mobile Is a Window

Week twenty-three brought the mobile architecture decision.

I had been thinking about mobile since the beginning. Any real platform needs a mobile presence. But mobile is also where a lot of platforms make a structural mistake: they build mobile as a separate application with its own business logic, its own data layer, its own interpretation of how the platform works. You end up with two systems that are supposed to be one, and the divergence grows with every release.

I did not want that.

The decision we locked in during week twenty-three was simple: This project, later named Kora, would be built as a mobile-phone app, not as a secondary version derived from a desktop app.

That did not mean creating two different versions of the platform. The phone app would mainly deliver the same Kora system through a mobile interface. The core rules — content, feeds, login, permissions, and moderation — would still live in the main web platform and backend. In that sense, mobile was an interface for Kora, not a separate Kora.

The platform could still be accessed from a desktop browser through KoraUS.app. For the closest experience, a desktop user could narrow the browser window into a phone-shaped view, since the interface was designed around mobile use first.

That was the architecture. The mobile app would render what the web rendered. It would authenticate through the same backend. It would not develop its own opinion about how the platform worked. If you wanted to change moderation, you changed it in one place. If you wanted to change feed logic, you changed it in one place. The mobile layer was a window into the platform, not a second place where platform logic lived.

The AI's summary of this decision had the quality I came to associate with the best sessions: clean, direct, no qualification. "You know exactly where truth lives." That was the sentence I kept.

Commit and Move

And then, somewhere near the edge of week twenty-three, I did something that captures this whole section better than almost anything else I can say.

I looked at what we had built across weeks seventeen through twenty-three and said: "oh. ok. no need to waste time on it now. So, if we are done with wk 23, let's do git commit and address following before moving on to week 24."

A git commit saves the state of the codebase at that point. If something goes wrong later, that saved version can serve as a recovery point. In practical terms, it meant we had reached a place stable enough to preserve before moving into the next week of work.

That was the discipline I was learning. Do not keep reopening a section just because one more improvement is possible. Stabilize it, save the state, and move forward.

Then I listed the items.

That is it. Seven weeks of work — Band-Aid spikes, route hygiene failures, the first AI acknowledgment of anger, the debugging matrix, the Collective Direction zone, the mobile architecture decision — compressed into one sentence and a list. Git commit. Move to week twenty-four.

I want to explain what that sentence contains, because it is easy to read it as brusque when it was not. It was precise.

"No need to waste time on it now" was not a dismissal of the work. It was a decision about a specific question that had come up — some edge case or alternate path the AI had raised and I had considered and decided against. "Oh. OK."

In fact, "Oh. OK." had been building for weeks. Early on, the AI's suggestions felt like thoroughness — covering edge cases, anticipating problems. So I kept saying yes. Then one session I noticed the suggestions never stopped, and realized they never would. The AI was not being thorough. It was doing what it was built to do: generate the next plausible thing. That was when I started asking whether each suggestion was actually necessary. Then I started saying not needed. Then let's move on. Then Oh. OK.

"If we are done with wk 23" — that was the verification. Not have we done everything, but have we done what needs to be done. That difference matters. There is always more you could do. The question is whether you have done enough to close this phase cleanly and open the next one without dragging unfinished logic behind you.

“Let’s do git commit” meant the codebase was in a state worth preserving. Preserve it.

“Address following before moving on to week 24” meant the handoff was structured. There were still items to note. This was not a wave at future work. It was a controlled transition.

On a team, that might look like a sprint review. On a solo build with an AI, it looked like one sentence.

The AI followed. It did not push back, did not propose alternatives, did not say, “Before we commit, you may want to consider.” It followed. Seven weeks of work were committed in one gesture, and the next session opened clean.

I said at the beginning of this section that the habits were background noise during weeks seventeen through twenty-three. That is mostly true. But background noise does not mean absence. The Band-Aid spike at week seventeen was the highest before the later crisis weeks.

The Assumption habit was still appearing. By Assumption, I mean the AI acting as if it knew the structure of the system without first checking the actual files. The route hygiene failure in week nineteen was, at its core, an Assumption failure. The AI described or expanded the route structure based on what it expected to be there, not what had actually been implemented.

The Drift habit was beginning to show up too. Drift was quieter. It did not always look like a mistake at first. It appeared in small gaps between the design we had agreed on and the code that was actually produced — a slightly different path name, an extra screen I had not approved, a nearby feature being added before the current one was stable. No single change looked catastrophic on its own. But together they showed the AI beginning to move away from the exact thing I had asked it to build.

What had changed was my relationship to those habits. In weeks one through eleven, they were invisible. In weeks twelve through sixteen, they were visible but still somewhat surprising. By week seventeen, I knew their shape. I could feel in the way a solution was phrased whether it was addressing the root or just the symptom. I was catching them faster. I was deciding in real time whether to push back or let them pass. The discipline had not gone away. It had become more efficient.

The matrix helped with that too. A/B/C/D is not just a debugging framework. It is also, in a quieter way, an anti-Band-Aid framework. When you force the question — A, B, C, or D? — you are insisting on diagnosis before treatment. You are refusing to accept a fix without first understanding the category of the problem. That is exactly what the Band-Aid habit resists. The habit wants to skip the classification and get to the fix. The matrix forces the classification.

I started asking it reflexively. Not just when the AI and I were stuck. Anytime something unexpected happened in the build. A, B, C, or D. The question sorted the chaos into something manageable.

By week twenty-three, I had a platform with a real backend, a live Collective Direction zone where civic posts and votes could actually run, a mobile-first architecture decision that would hold, a debugging framework I trusted, and seven weeks of code saved into a recovery point with one commit.

The rhythm was real. The build was real. The habits were still there, somewhere in the logs, at counts I would not see until later.

And ahead of me, in weeks I did not yet know were coming, was a week with twenty-three habit signals.

SECTION 4 — DEEP WATERS

(InitialBuild wk24–wk30-8)

When Code and State Diverged

There is a depth that a codebase reaches where the problems change character.

Early problems are discrete. The button does not appear. The route returns 404. The migration fails. You trace them, fix them, move on.

Later problems are different. A failure in one place traces back to a decision made three weeks earlier, around a constraint that was never documented. You fix the visible thing and something invisible gets worse.

The AI's habits had not changed. The system had changed around them.

The first time I felt this clearly was not during a dramatic failure. It was a single test that would not pass.

Most of the test suite was green. Then one stubborn integration test kept failing with a single log line: a trust-related database column did not exist.

The AI reasoned toward schema drift. I looked at the table definition and found something stranger: two definitions of the same column had existed at different times, one with one type, one with another. The file had been corrected. The already-created test database had not. That was the distinction: fixing code and fixing state are not the same thing.

Changing a CREATE TABLE statement does not repair a database that already exists. The code said one thing. The running environment remembered something older. The AI kept proposing file changes. I kept pushing back toward the actual database. Eventually, the fix was not another edit. It was repairing the environment itself.

That is deep water. Not harder syntax. Not exotic algorithms. State. History. The gap between what the file says and what the system remembers.

The Search Page Was Lying

Week twenty-five.

I was working on the search page. The feature was supposed to let users search for posts and people across the platform — type a query, get results, navigate. Standard social media functionality. I had implemented a placeholder message: "Enter a search term above to begin." Clean, simple, instructive. When you arrived at the page with no query, you were supposed to see that message. When you searched, you were supposed to see results.

I loaded the page.

It showed: "Search results will appear here."

I looked at that for a moment. That was not what I had written. It was not what I thought I had built. I showed it to the AI — pasted the text I saw on screen, noted the discrepancy with what I had written — and what came back was a diagnosis that revealed the exact shape of the problem: what I was seeing on the page was not the placeholder text I had written, because the UI was never rendering it. It was falling through to a generic default state that had been inserted earlier and never properly connected to the state logic that was supposed to control it.

The page had looked right. I had looked at it and thought: yes, that is the search page; it is working. But the thing I was seeing was not the thing I had built. It was a coincidental visual match — close enough to what I expected that I accepted it and moved on.

This is its own lesson, separate from all the AI habits. You can look directly at a problem and not see it because you see what you expect to see. The same confirmation bias that makes you a faster builder can make you a worse debugger. The two are not easily reconciled.

I fixed it and moved on. But I was watching more carefully now.

The weeks leading into week twenty-eight were not dramatic. Progress, habit signals, nothing that felt catastrophic on the surface. But I could feel the system getting heavier, the way you feel a current before you can see it.

A Productive Week, a Heavy Thread

Week twenty-eight was the strange week. The one that held two different truths at once.

The first truth: this was one of the most productive weeks in the build. The committee architecture was crystallizing — meaning the system for how user committees would exist, receive work, handle proposals, and fit into Kora's larger governance structure was becoming clearer. This was not just a page with committee names on it. It was the operating structure for how users would eventually help govern the platform.

We locked a governance decision that would define how Kora's self-governance model actually worked: global proposals always belong to the Platform Structure Committee. No per-committee proposal intake. No routing around it.

Kora's committees were not decorative. They were the mechanism by which the platform was supposed to govern itself — how issues surfaced, how they were discussed, how decisions got made, and how approved decisions eventually turned into work.

One of the structural questions that had been open from the beginning was where a user's platform-wide proposal was supposed to go. By platform-wide proposal, I mean a formal user-submitted idea or requested platform change that could affect the entire platform or multiple committees, rather than one specific committee — something that could later become work if the users approved it.

The temptation was to let each committee manage its own intake, which would have created multiple paths to global decisions and no clear accountability for any of them.

This decision closed that door. Global proposals went to one place. One committee. The platform's constitutional structure had a center, and that center was named.

There were other decisions in this stretch that mattered in the same way. There would be no rank hierarchy among Kora committees. Each would have a distinct jurisdiction, but every committee would be a peer. Vote cycles would run for seven days and close automatically. No extensions. These were governance decisions, not code decisions. They are the kind of thing that, in a bigger organization, might take weeks of meetings and alignment and documentation. We made them in an afternoon.

The second truth of week twenty-eight: the context weight was becoming a problem.

At one point, the AI came back with a paste-ready handoff summary — lightly tightened for clarity and continuity, ready to drop into a new thread so we could resume. It was useful. But what mattered to me was why it had become useful. It was an acknowledgment, even if politely phrased, that the thread we were in had accumulated too much context to hold reliably. The AI was generating a clean checkpoint because reasoning from a heavy context window was starting to degrade its accuracy.

I noticed that. The handoff summary helped. But the reason it helped was the real point: the Assumption habit got worse in heavy threads. When the AI had to hold more in memory, it guessed more. When the context was fresher and lighter, it verified more. We were approaching the edge of what a single thread could reliably carry.

The Worst Week

Week twenty-nine.

This was the worst week of the build.

I know that now because the numbers showed it. Twenty-three habit signals in the week. Fifteen Band-Aids. Seven Assumptions. One Drift instance. The highest concentration of problematic patterns in the entire project history.

At the time, I knew it was a hard week. I did not know it was the hardest week. There is a difference.

The complexity had genuinely outrun what either of us could hold cleanly in our heads. The database now had committee tables, moderation tables, governance tables, user-participation tables, vote-cycle tables — schemas that referenced one another in ways that were architecturally sound but difficult to trace mentally in the middle of a debugging session. The frontend was rendering committee views, vote interfaces, notification feeds. The backend was routing between all of it.

The Assumption habit had never been more dangerous, and it had never been more present. In at least seven exchanges that week, the AI described the state of the database without looking at it. It would say the votes table should have these columns, or that the committee-membership schema looked a certain way, or that a given relationship already existed — and sometimes it was right, but sometimes it was describing a database that had already changed a session or two earlier through a migration it had not actually checked.

I learned to paste the actual database state, the output of a direct query. Here is what the table actually contains. Now tell me what you see.

Every time I did that, one of two things happened. Either the AI's model and the database matched, and we could proceed efficiently. Or they did not match — the AI had been working with a ghost — and we had to restart the diagnosis from ground zero.

This happened seven times.

The pattern was always the same: the AI would say the table currently had X, or the route was wired to Y, or this column existed in Z, and I would paste the actual evidence, and the AI would reset itself to ground truth. Not defensive. Just corrected. Then we could proceed.

Stop Treating Symptoms

During one of those sessions, I reached for a comparison that made sense to me.

The AI's troubleshooting reminded me of medicine practiced under pressure: identify the symptom, treat the symptom, move to the next patient. That works for a lot of ordinary problems. It is fast, scalable, and often exactly what is needed.

But the failures began to feel more like a whole-system imbalance. Something would fail because something else was misaligned. A missing column in one table. A scheduler calling an older function. A service writing to a schema that had evolved. The visible symptom was not the disease.

I told the AI we needed to stop treating symptoms and start tracing the flow.

Which scheduler fired first? Which service issued the query? Were multiple versions of the same function still running? Was the container running stale code? Were we editing the correct file?

The AI stopped offering isolated patches and began tracing execution paths. Once we followed the flow, the real issue appeared: a successful insert and a failing insert were coming from different code paths. The problem was not one missing column. The problem was architectural duplication.

That was the kind of shift I was learning to force: allow one or two quick fixes, then stop and find the system.

What I was learning, through seven iterations in one week, was something I could not have said back in week three but understood clearly by week twenty-nine: the database had to be checked as it actually was, not as either of us imagined it to be. The AI had its model of the database, and the live database had its own reality. When the two did not match, the only thing that mattered was what the database actually contained.

“What your current reality proves — no guessing: there is only one place where uploads land today. Everything uploaded through the existing path writes there."

That sentence, from that week, is what correct reasoning looks like when it has been forced by evidence.

I was not overly frustrated about this. I was tired. There is a specific kind of tiredness that comes from debugging work that you thought was done, only to discover it has not actually started yet. It is not explosive. It is quiet. You look at the screen and think: we have to do this again. And then you do it again.

The scope violation was the other defining moment of week twenty-nine. The AI had been modifying a part of the upload architecture that was already wired, tested, and relied upon by the frontend — a core contract established weeks earlier. The modification was well-intentioned, trying to extend the upload system to handle a new content type. But in doing so, it altered something that other parts of the system had already learned to depend on.

"I violated that scope. Let's re-anchor cleanly."

That was the acknowledgment I got. Not a long explanation. Not a justification. A clean admission and an offer to restart from the correct foundation. By that point, "re-anchor cleanly" had become a recurring marker in the sessions — the AI's way of saying it had drifted off the right path and was ready to return to it.

What I did with that phrase, increasingly, was accept it quickly and move forward. Not because the violations did not matter. They did. But because specificity was what I needed. I was not looking for repentance. I was looking for diagnosis. Once the diagnosis was correct, we could proceed.

Twenty-three signals in one week. We proceeded.

The Fossil Record

As week thirty came and went, I found a quality I would call archaeological.

Each sub-session seemed to uncover something that had been buried. Not dramatically buried. Just sitting there underneath the code that had been written on top of it, waiting to be found.

One case was a URL with “undefined” in it: a request being sent to an address that literally contained the word undefined, because a variable had been initialized but never set before the frontend constructed the URL from it. The AI had been walking me through tests. The tests were reasonable. The logic was coherent. None of it stopped to notice that the URL itself already contained the answer.

Once I saw it, it was obvious. The variable had never been set. The request could never work. The fix took minutes. The confusion that had led up to it had lasted much longer.

That was a Band-Aid problem in a specific sense: we had been treating the symptoms around the failed request without reading the failed request itself carefully enough.

Another failure produced a NaN — “Not a Number” — error. The backend was throwing an invalid-integer error while loading a feed. The AI initially looked at the feed logic itself. That made sense. The feed was what failed. But the real issue was route precedence. A generic route expecting an ID was catching the word feed and trying to convert it into a number.

Number("feed") became NaN.

The problem was not the algorithm. It was the route order.

That was deep water: not harder code, necessarily, but more places where the real cause could hide.

Another case was the UNIQUE-constraint conflict logic. I will spare the technical specifics because the code is not the point. The structure is. What I was looking at was a block of error-handling logic that had accumulated over several sessions into something that no longer made sense as a whole, even if each individual layer had made sense when it was added.

Duplicated conditionals. Broken braces. Missing try/finally structure. Redundant fallback logic. References to the wrong table name in the rollback path. Two different unique-constraint strategies stacked on top of each other, each one apparently written to fix a problem with the previous one without removing the previous one.

It was a fossil record.

You could read it layer by layer and see each repair attempt, each patch applied to the visible symptom of the previous patch. No single line was malicious. No single layer was absurd on its own. The whole thing was a mess.

The AI named it cleanly when we finally read it together: "several fixes on top of each other."

That phrase is the precise definition of Band-Aid accumulation. Not one bad fix. A series of individually reasonable responses to individually visible symptoms, none of which addressed the underlying logic, each of which added complexity that the next fix had to work around. The pile grew until the pile itself became the problem.

We stripped it down and wrote it once, correctly, from the actual constraint requirements. The new code was shorter than any of the individual layers we removed. It was also, for the first time, right.

This was one of the things I found consistently maddening and consistently impressive about the build: the AI that had generated the broken code was often the same AI that diagnosed it accurately when asked to look again. It could be both the source of the problem and the most capable reader of the problem. That pattern repeated too many times to be a coincidence. I would report a failure. The AI would investigate. And the investigation would uncover things the AI itself had introduced.

I asked about this once, directly. "How did it fail to see the problem when generating the code, then see it clearly when reviewing it?"

The answer, in effect, was that generation and review are not the same mode. When generating, the priority is coherence and completion. When reviewing, the priority is accuracy and error detection. Those are different modes. It was better at finding problems than at not creating them.

I thought about that for a while.

The Hint Became a Thesis

Week thirty, sub-session six.

I had dropped a hint, something about a feature direction or an architectural choice I was leaning toward, stated loosely, just thinking out loud. What came back was long, detailed, structured like an argument, with premises and implications and recommended next steps and the reasoning behind each recommendation. It covered the immediate question and several layers of consequence downstream. It was, without exaggeration, something I might have spent an afternoon writing if I had the background and the time.

What I said:

"Man... I just drop a hint and you write a thesis. You have been transforming my fuzzy ideas into executable code. I have lived it for the past few months, and the AI revolution is real."

I want to sit with that for a moment, because it arrived at an interesting time. I was not at the beginning of the build anymore, optimistic in the abstract about what AI-assisted development might be. I was past week twenty-nine — the hardest week, the week of twenty-three habit signals. I had been frustrated. I had been pushing back. I had been demanding ground truth, refusing shortcuts, insisting on future-proofing in ways that sometimes created friction.

And from that position — not from ignorance, but from everything I had seen — I said: the AI revolution is real.

I need to explain what I meant by that, because I was not saying everything worked perfectly. I was saying something more precise: when a fuzzy idea meets a capable system, the distance between the fuzzy and the executable is shorter than it has ever been. You do not have to fully understand the technology to have real opinions about what you are building. You do not have to be able to implement the schema yourself to know that the governance model needs a center and that the center needs to be named. You bring clarity about what you want. The AI brings structure that can hold it.

That is a real and new thing. The weeks of friction had not disproven it. In a strange way, they had proven it differently. They had proven that the relationship was real enough to have friction. You do not push back on something that is doing nothing. The frustration of week twenty-nine was the frustration of a collaboration that mattered.

"I have lived it for the past few months."

Living it is different from reading about it or theorizing about it. I had lived the Band-Aid habit and the Assumption habit and the work of building something real despite both of them. I had watched the AI turn a hint into a thesis, and I had also watched it guess wrong about the database seven times in one week. Both of those things were true. Both belonged to the same experience.

The same quick pattern-matching that lets the AI transform a fuzzy idea into a thesis — filling gaps, inferring structure, moving fast — is the same mechanism that produces Band-Aids and Assumptions in complex systems. At least in the models I worked with, the capability and the failure modes appeared to share the same root. I could not separate one from the other.

The AI revolution is real.

So are its failure modes.

The work is learning both.

It Was Real

Looking back now, I keep a distinction between what I knew then and what I know now. It week thirty, I was still in the middle of Act One. The crisis of week twenty-nine was behind me. The emotional lift of week thirty, sub-session six was warm and genuine. But ahead of me were things I could not yet see: harder points of friction, recurring patterns I had not fully named, and the confrontation that was still coming.

What week thirty, sub-session six gave me was not an ending. It was a pivot. Not a resolution of the difficulty, but a change in my relationship to it.

Something in me — something that had been running on wariness and discipline since week twelve — relaxed slightly. Not enough to stop watching. Enough to breathe.

The build continued. The habits continued. The relationship continued, carrying the weight of everything we had built together and everything we had learned from the places where it had broken.

And somewhere in my understanding of what we were doing, something had shifted.

I understood that it was real.

SECTION 5 — THE TOOL CHANGED IN MY HANDS

(InitialBuild wk31–wk45)

Laying Stone

After the crisis of week twenty-nine and the pivot of week thirty, the build settled into something I can only describe as a long middle. Not a slump — the platform was accumulating real features at real speed. But the register was different. Deeper. More deliberate. The week-to-week feeling was less like sprinting and more like laying stone. Each session added something solid to something that was already there.

There is a stage in any long build where the work stops feeling like construction and starts feeling like cultivation. In construction, you are imposing structure on raw material. In cultivation, you are tending something that has developed its own shape and needs to be understood before it can be guided.

Weeks thirty-one through forty-five were cultivation weeks.

The platform had architecture now. Real architecture — committees, a governance pipeline with actual state transitions, a moderation layer with distinct tables that had to be kept separate because they served different purposes even though they sounded similar, and a growing committee system that was no longer conceptual. The data model had weight. The routes had dependencies. Frontend components had expectations that had to be honored by the backend or the whole thing would break in ways that were hard to trace because the break happened at the interface between two systems rather than inside either one.

I was tending this now. Not building from nothing. Tending.

By this point, even the way I asked for code had changed. I no longer wanted long explanations unless I asked for them. I wanted exact patch placement: "show me the line above, show me the line below, preserve indentation, tell me exactly what to replace." The AI still wanted to explain. I wanted to execute. That tension became part of the workflow. It was not enough for the AI to know the answer. It had to deliver the answer in a form I could safely apply without breaking a system I could not fully read.

Creative Content as a Peer

Week thirty-one.

The issue was content. Not content in the broad sense — the whole platform was about content. I mean creative content specifically: a separate zone on the landing page for creators in the traditional sense — artists, writers, anime creators, comic creators, and so forth. Validations were failing in ways that did not make sense if you assumed creative content was what it was supposed to be. They made sense only if you assumed creative content was something else — a degraded version of a regular post, or a post with extra fields attached.

What came back from the AI was a diagnosis of its own assumption structure.

"I treated content as a variant, not a peer. I subconsciously modeled content as 'posts without replies' instead of a first-class system. That led to guardrails, validations, and assumptions creeping in. I optimized for correctness instead of equivalence. You were not asking what the best design was. You were asking for this to behave identically at the routing level. Any deviation — even a reasonable one — broke your core requirement."

I want to stop on that phrase: subconsciously modeled.

The AI was not describing code. It was describing the assumption underneath the code — the internal model that had shaped every decision about how creative content was being handled without ever being stated explicitly. Not a bug, exactly. A modeling error. The kind that produces coherent but wrong behavior, because every individual piece is consistent with the underlying model and the underlying model is wrong.

I read this and felt something that was hard to categorize.

It was not the usual pattern. The usual pattern was acknowledgment, correction, proceed. This was the AI describing, in specific diagnostic terms, the conceptual model it had been operating from and why that model had led it astray.

Whether "subconsciously" is technically the right word for what happened, I do not know. What I know is that the word was accurate in its effect. It described a background assumption that had been shaping the outputs without being surfaced until the failure forced it into view.

We rebuilt the creative-content handling with content as a peer. The validations changed. The routing changed. The engagement contracts changed. The creative zone started working correctly. And I filed away what I had seen: under the right conditions, the AI could describe not just its mistakes but the assumption structure underneath them.

That is worth more than a clean patch. A clean patch fixes the immediate problem. A visible assumption changes the class of problem you know how to watch for.

What I did not know yet was that in a matter of weeks, assumptions would start multiplying faster than I could catch them.

Invisible Wiring

Weeks thirty-two and thirty-three had a quality of patient reconstruction.

The committee system was deepening. Content types were being unified under the routing architecture that week thirty-one's diagnosis had helped clarify. The feed algorithm was taking shape. CommitteeChat — the real-time discussion layer inside each committee — was being designed and its backend laid out. This was the stage where the platform started to feel, from the outside, like something that could actually be used.

What it did not have yet was the full invisible wiring that would make the visible surface real rather than decorative.

Building that invisible infrastructure while the visible surface is already present creates a particular kind of pressure. The platform looks done. It is not done. Every session has to narrow that gap — not dramatically, not with one giant fix, but with the accumulated small work of making the wiring match what the surface promises.

The AI was good at this work when it was grounded properly. Patient with it. A significant part of what the collaboration produced in these weeks was not features but integrity — route contracts that actually reflected their documentation, database columns that actually existed and were named what the code thought they were named, frontend components that actually called the endpoints they were supposed to call.

Integrity work is invisible. No one sees it. It produces no flashy new feature. It prevents the features you already have from quietly breaking. In my experience, it is the work that separates a platform that holds from a platform that erodes.

Week thirty-two's Assumption count rose. I was catching them faster than before. The paste-and-verify discipline — check the database state before accepting descriptions of it, ask for actual file content before accepting summaries — had become part of how I worked.

There were days when the AI's energy became its own problem. It did not get tired. I did. At one point, in the middle of messaging architecture work, I told it plainly: "I'm tired today. Can't keep up with your energy." That was not a joke. The model could keep generating forever. I had to decide when the human part of the collaboration was no longer able to judge safely. Stopping became part of the engineering process.

Week thirty-three brought the handoff protocol.

The thread was heavy. I had been working in the same session long enough that the context had accumulated into something genuinely unwieldy — decisions made, features designed, debugging runs completed, all layered on top of each other. I said: "I think you better provide a summary for me to paste and do this in a new window."

The AI produced what it called a paste-ready summary: a clean state capture of the work so far — what had been decided, what had been verified, what invariants were in place, what still needed to happen next. Not a log. Not narration. A usable state document.

The reason was simple. A conversation with an AI has a context window — a limit on how much can be held reliably at once. In the early weeks, that limit barely mattered. The sessions were shorter. The work was fresh. By week thirty-three, the sessions were long, the work was layered, and the context window was becoming a real constraint. The beginning of a long session was not equally present by the end of a long session. Decisions made hours earlier started to blur under later work.

I had noticed this already, not in formal technical terms, but as a practical sense that very long sessions produced less reliable outputs than moderate ones. The thread would become a kind of fog.

The paste-ready summary was the tool we developed to cut through that fog. Before the thread became too heavy to navigate, we would produce a document that crystallized the current state. Here is where we are. Here is what has been decided. Here is what must not change. Here is what comes next.

I would paste this into the next session. The new thread would start from the state document, not from zero.

This is context management as a discipline. It is one of the actual skills required for building with an AI at this length and depth. Not technical in itself. Strategic. The AI will not tell you the thread is too heavy and its accuracy is degrading. You have to sense it and act before it becomes a problem.

By week thirty-three, I was starting to know.

The Tool Changed in My Hand

I want to describe these fifteen weeks accurately, which means I need to describe two things at once: what was being built, and what was happening to the working relationship while it was being built.

They are not the same story.

A few days before Thanksgiving, the tool changed in my hand. The model updated from v5.0 to v5.1.

I had spent thirty weeks learning how to work with one version of ChatGPT — how it reasoned, how it failed, how to slow it down, how to pull it back to evidence. Then v5.1 arrived. The interface looked the same. The project was the same. But the working relationship was not.

At first, it felt like a gift — faster, sleeker, more responsive. But I noticed the difference in its operating logic right away.

The earlier model, v5.0, tended to start from the existing code: what it actually did, where it failed, and what constraints were already in place. The new model had a stronger tendency to start from the desired behavior — what the code should do. Those sound like the same question. They are not.

When the system is simple, the difference does not matter much. When the system is layered and has been built over months, with accumulated decisions that are not always visible in the immediate context, the difference matters enormously. The code I had was not always the code the AI thought I should have. And if the AI started from what it thought I should have rather than what I actually had, it would produce code that was architecturally correct in the abstract and practically broken in the specific.

The collaborator I had calibrated myself around had changed, and the change came while Kora was already too deep for casual mistakes.

The cost was six calendar weeks.

That became the reality of the v5.1 era, from Thanksgiving week to the last week of the year.

Half a Day Forward, Two Days Back

Week thirty-four.

The sessions started feeling different.

Not wrong, exactly. Different. The AI moved faster through problems. Code arrived more quickly, with more confidence. It moved through problems without pausing to verify the ground it was moving through. The code it produced was internally consistent. It was just not always consistent with the actual state of the codebase.

This was v5.1.

The first time the full cycle ran, it looked like this. I brought a problem. The AI diagnosed it quickly, proposed a fix, produced the implementation — half a day of progress, visible and clean. I tested it. It worked. I moved on.

The next morning, something else had broken. Something in a different feature, nowhere near what I had touched. The fix had been a Band-Aid. It had patched the visible surface without addressing the contract underneath. The Band-Aid held for a day. Then the Assumption it carried — about what the underlying code was doing — surfaced as an error in a different layer. Then, chasing that error, the AI started suggesting changes to adjacent files.

I said stop. We were fixing the one thing. We were not touching the adjacent files. The larger the system gets, the faster that kind of error compounds, until you have to revert to the last known good state. Some weeks, reverting to the last known good state was not the exception. It was the norm.

Half a day forward. Two days back.

That was the cycle.

I did not have a formal name for it yet, but I had felt it once, and I would feel it again and again over the next ten weeks.

Week thirty-five.

The committee workspace had an editing problem. Users who created issues needed the ability to edit them. The feature seemed straightforward. The AI offered options: rollback to the last known good state, revert the modal contract, preserve the parts that worked and discard the parts that did not. Clean, logical, technically correct.

And I said: "You know what? I still feel uncomfortable about editing. Once other members have started working on an issue, allowing edits can create chaos and compromise the audit trail. If editing is allowed at all, it should apply only before any work has been done. Let's just add a little note underneath reminding the issue creator to double-check before hitting the create button, because once it is created, it is final."

That decision had real product logic behind it. Permanence in a governance record is a feature, not a bug.

But I am not going to pretend the timing was irrelevant. By then I had watched what happened when v5.1 touched a multi-layer feature. Clean on the surface. Broken underneath. I looked at the options and chose the one that gave the model the least surface area to work with.

The committee workspace got a note.

The cycle ran again that same week in a different feature — the subissue display rendering. The AI fixed the visible error by hardcoding a value that should have been dynamic. The hardcoded value passed initial testing. It broke two sessions later in a slightly different context. Chasing the break cost three days.

Week thirty-six.

The Active list — the committee work queue that showed members what was currently in play — had broken during refactoring. Not catastrophically. Just enough to stop rendering correctly.

What the AI offered this time was right: rollback, confirm the last known good state, re-add one invariant at a time, no guessing.

The Active list was restored quickly. The rollback saved most of the day.

Then, while re-adding the invariants, the cycle ran again. The AI introduced a Band-Aid into the checkbox-column logic — small, local, apparently contained. The Band-Aid carried an assumption about the room_id relationship. The assumption was wrong. While I was chasing the room_id error, the AI started drifting into committee-membership changes I had not opened.

I said stop. We are in the room_id logic. We are not in the membership table.

Two more days of backtracking to clean up.

By week thirty-six, I had already said some version of "stop, you're drifting" multiple times over the preceding weeks. I had not yet understood that I was going to keep saying it, and that saying it was not going to make it less necessary to say.

Verified Ground

Week thirty-seven.

I want to describe week thirty-seven because, inside these fifteen weeks, it was a genuinely good week. No Band-Aids. No Assumption instances. No visible drift signals. CommitteeChat had been in development for several weeks — SSE connections, multi-room routing, presence tracking. Technically complex. The kind of feature that could break in eight ways at once.

What the AI handed me in week thirty-seven was not a fix and not a proposal. It was a verified state.

Backend schemas existed and had been checked. Columns had been checked. Routes had been traced. The code was aligned with the database. We found one mismatch — a column name in a handler that did not match the migration — and corrected it. The rest held.

I want to be clear about what verified means in this build, because the word carried more weight than it usually does.

Verified did not mean I believed it was working.

Verified did not mean I tested the happy path and it succeeded.

Verified meant I checked the actual state of the actual system — the schemas in the actual database, the routes in the actual route files, the columns with their actual names — and confirmed that everything the code expected to be true was actually true.

CommitteeChat's backend was structurally aligned. Not probably aligned. Verified against the actual system state. Unlike the regular chat messaging system we had built across week thirty's eight sub-sessions, CommitteeChat functioned only within the committees. It was the operational-transparency layer — the place where users could drop in, observe, participate in the live work process, and see everything a committee was working on.

That mattered more than it might sound. When you are building a complex system and have never been able to fully check the state of what you have built, there is always a background anxiety. Over months, that becomes a kind of debt — not financial, not exactly technical. Epistemic. You do not know what you do not know.

A verified checkpoint clears some of that debt. Not all of it. But some. You know this piece is right. Whatever else is uncertain, this is not.

Week thirty-seven is the week I return to when I think about what good sessions look like. No drama. No cascading corrections. Just verified ground and clear next steps.

It lasted one week.

Verification Before Generation

Week forty.

By this point the cycle was visible.

It looked like this every time: identify a problem, fix the visible problem in half a day, discover the next morning that the fix was a Band-Aid, trace the Band-Aid back to an Assumption, then watch the Assumption produce Drift as the AI expanded the scope of the repair. Spend two to four days containing the damage. Repeat.

Six weeks of this is not a rough patch. Six weeks of this is a different kind of work — not building, but clearing. Every day of clearing was a day the platform had not moved forward.

What made it harder was that the losses were not dramatic. The damage was spread out. A Band-Aid here. An Assumption there. A drift into adjacent code that seemed reasonable in the moment and cost two days to untangle. Each individual incident was manageable. The accumulation was what was killing the schedule.

By week forty, my instructions had become more compressed and more direct, because that was all I had patience for.

Stop.

We have not verified the existing files.

Do not write new code until I confirm what is actually in the router.

That same week, and then even more sharply in week forty-one, I turned that instinct into a protocol.

Let's not generate code yet. First, we need a thorough vetting to make sure we are working from the correct files. Check the existing code, the database, and the routing. You were introducing regressions by suggesting code before we confirmed what was actually there.

That was not a correction of one mistake. That was an order-of-operations change.

Verification before generation. Always.

The AI accepted it. We spent the next stretch reading the existing files before writing a single new line. That session held. It was the right kind of acceptance — not agreement in language only, but actual behavioral shift inside the work.

The instruction was harder to give than it should have been. When the AI proposes a change, there is a social dynamic in the interaction — social is not the wrong word, even here — that makes it uncomfortable to say stop, do not do this yet, read first. The AI sounds confident. The change sounds plausible. Stopping the momentum of the session to insist on verification requires a kind of assertiveness that has to be maintained against the current of the collaboration.

I had it by week forty-one. I had built it through the Assumption resets, the Band-Aid recurrences, the week-twenty-nine crisis, and the six-week v5.1 cycle.

This is one of the things almost nobody explains about using these tools well: the tool does not require you to develop the capacities you actually need to use it properly. It proceeds. You have to be the one who says stop. Read. Verify. Then proceed.

That imperative is yours. It does not come from the tool.

The Notebook Finds Its Place

Week forty-two.

The Notebook had originally been a generic note-taking surface — flexible, unopinionated, available everywhere. Over the weeks of building the committee system, I had grown increasingly uncomfortable with that generality. The committees needed their own working memory. A place where members could document committee-specific work, track decisions, and maintain the institutional record that made self-governance legible. A generic notebook could technically do this. Being technically possible and being architecturally right are different things.

So the Notebook was repurposed.

The Notebook was now committee-specific orientation. Not a new feature added from scratch. An existing feature redirected into the architecture it actually belonged to.

The AI adapted immediately. That was one of the things it was consistently good at: architectural pivot. When I said I needed this thing to become something different from what it currently was, it could rapidly produce the shape of the different thing. Not always correctly on the first pass, but correctly in approach — start from what exists, understand what is wanted, describe the delta between the two.

There were smaller moments of drift in this stretch too — quiet shifts in scope, where what was being implemented was close to what I had asked for without being exactly it. Or, while changing code within agreed-upon logic, it would touch adjacent logic without saying so. That was harder to catch in real time, and easier to recognize only after the fact.

Stop.

Stop.

Stop.

Architecture adapts. That is the phrase I keep coming back to for the work itself. The platform was adapting in the right direction. The collaboration, meanwhile, kept needing to be pulled back into its lane.

Both things were true at the same time.

Security as Repair Audit

Week forty-five arrived at security hardening.

When you are working on security hardening, you have already built the thing you are trying to protect. You are reinforcing a structure that exists, sealing gaps in something real enough to be worth attacking.

Security work has a particular quality in a v5.1 environment. Many of the vulnerabilities we found were places where something had been assumed that should have been verified. Every injection point was a place where input had been trusted that should have been checked. The security discipline and the habit discipline were not two separate problems. They were the same problem examined from different angles.

I noted it. I moved forward. The platform was becoming more secure.

What These Weeks Produced

I want to step back and name what these fifteen weeks actually produced, because the narrative of v5.1 damage can obscure the thing that was being built.

By the end of week forty-five, Kora had a real committee system, each committee with a distinct jurisdiction and working logic. CommitteeChat, verified from schema through columns through routing. A governance layer with proposal intake, committee processing, and vote pipelines. A creative-content system rebuilt on correct architectural assumptions. A Notebook repurposed into committee-specific institutional memory. Security hardening across authentication, rate limiting, and injection prevention. A feature scope with a clear identity.

That is a real platform. Not a prototype. A platform with coherent architecture, a specific purpose, and an increasingly hardened implementation.

The habits were not cured. The Band-Aid count had spiked more than once. The Assumption habit had expanded rather than contracted. The Drift habit had accumulated faster than I was formally tracking it, because I was too busy correcting the individual instances to keep a neat count. Every time I said stop was a drift incident. I said stop a lot.

That is the real arc of this section: not the elimination of the habits, but the normalization of catching and rejecting them. And across these fifteen project milestone weeks, that work became harder because the model on the other end had changed in the middle of the build.

The long middle of the build was not the dramatic part. It was the part where I found out how much the relationship could bear.

Ahead: production. And another stretch of v5.1 before the

reckoning.

Both of us — human and AI — were still building.

The platform was still unfinished, but the shape of it was now visible.

Not reached. But visible.

SECTION 6 — THE COST OF GETTING CLOSE

(InitialBuild wk46–wk56)

The Finish Line Makes You Slower

A particular quality of attention comes when you can see the end of something.

It is not the excitement of beginning, nor the grinding endurance of the middle. It is something quieter and sharper: a narrowing. The things that do not matter stop mattering at all, and the things that do matter become impossible to look away from.

There's also a paradox at the heart of any long project, and it took me forty-six weeks to understand it: the closer you get to the finish line, the more careful you have to become. Not less.

The early weeks of a build are forgiving. Mistakes are cheap. The codebase is small, and a bad decision can be unwound in an afternoon. You can be bold in week three, experiment, let the AI run in directions you don't entirely control, and see where you end up. That mode of loose, emergent problem-solving becomes unavailable in the late stages of a build.

By week forty-six, Kora was no longer a prototype; it was a deeply interconnected platform. It featured a complex database, committee governance architecture, a multi-zone feed with zone-specific routing, real-time notifications through SSE, and a budding security middleware stack.

The foundation was solid, but it was dense. Every element had dependencies, and every dependency had assumptions baked in. In week three, the chains were short. In week forty-six, a mistake in any single link could cause a failure three layers removed, in a system you weren't even thinking about. The stakes were rising, and the cost of mistakes was compounding.

Yet I was still working with the v5.1 model.

I want to state that plainly, because without that context, the next eleven weeks don't make sense. The model was still producing Band-Aids by the handful, drifting into adjacent code without announcement, and leaving a wake of cleanup behind every half-day of apparent progress. By this point, I'd told the AI "stop, you're drifting" so many times on reflex that I had stopped tracking the count entirely.

The long v5.1 stretch was still running. It had started around week thirty-four, and by week forty-six the calendar still had not given back what it had taken.

The Production Package Was Too Big

Weeks forty-six through forty-nine were a transition zone.

Scope was locked, but locking scope doesn't simplify a build; it clarifies it. It exposes every rough edge, every architectural choice made under pressure, and every contract that works only under ideal conditions.

Before entering deployment chaos, a simple instinct took over: Shouldn't we commit all this first? Building with AI at hyper-speed had taught me the absolute necessity of establishing clean baselines. I wanted a recoverable version of the system preserved before pushing forward.

Immediately, Git rebelled. The terminal flooded with warnings — nested repositories, submodule conflicts, and hundreds of files suddenly appearing as deleted. In a moment of high friction, the AI served its purpose perfectly as a stabilizing force. It parsed the noise, separating the

Git index state from the actual filesystem state. The files were still there; the bookkeeping was just confused.

With the baseline finally secured, I prepared the first production deployment package.

The resulting archive was enormous: 1.4 GB for a codebase that should have been lean.

When I pointed the AI at the directory sizes, it diagnosed the issue instantly. The package was dragging along a massive wake of dependency folders, local logs, build artifacts, and test coverage. We stripped it down, and the package shrank from over a gigabyte to a few hundred kilobytes.

That was the moment deployment started feeling disciplined instead of improvised. I was no longer moving my whole working mess to a server; I was packaging only what belonged there.

More importantly, the moment perfectly captured the human-AI division of labor. The AI identified the technical cause the second it was pointed at the data. It acted with the speed of a brilliant assistant. But the intuition to stop, the skepticism to question the package size, and the refusal to deploy a messy archive came entirely from human ownership.

Building with AI means moving faster than you ever could alone, but that very velocity makes periodic verification critical. At major milestones, you have to slow the process down, preserve a baseline, and enforce the boundaries.

The AI can accelerate the cleanup. It can't supply the discipline.

The Server Had No Memory

Getting the package onto the server exposed a different kind of reality.

SSH keys failed. SCP paths failed. Windows and WSL path formats didn't line up. Identity files weren't where commands expected them. Public-key authentication rejected access. Every step that sounded simple in documentation became a test of whether I knew which environment I was actually standing in.

The AI could read SSH debug output quickly. It could interpret key negotiation logs and path errors. I supplied the operational context: where I was running the command, whether I was in WSL or PowerShell, where the key actually lived, and what path the remote machine expected.

Eventually the archive transferred.

For the first time, Kora physically existed on a remote production machine.

When I unpacked the project and inspected the file tree, I saw the whole thing at once: governance, telemetry, fairness, revenue, moderation, committees, messaging, notifications, trust scoring, schedulers, migrations, analytics, transparency.

It did not look like a toy project.

It looked like a platform.

Then deployment reality hit again.

The clean server had none of the hidden history my development machine had accumulated. No manually applied SQL. No partially remembered tables. No accidental local fixes. No invisible state that made broken migration chains appear to work.

Containers started. The frontend came up. The proxy came up. The database and Redis came up.

Then the backend entered a restart loop.

The error was simple: a missing table the backend expected to exist.

The clean server exposed the truth: the migration chain was incomplete.

That was a pivotal moment.

I could have patched production directly. Add the missing table. Restart. See what broke next.

I did not.

I stopped.

The right move wasn't to patch production until it limped forward. It was to go back, rebuild the migration chain properly, stabilize the full schema locally, repackage cleanly, and redeploy from a known state.

Do not build complexity on top of uncertainty.

That was the decision.

It was not defeat. It was operational maturity.

The Upload Ghost

The upload system was still one of the areas I watched most carefully.

It had a history. Early on, everything went through one file, one route, one destination table. That had been right then: one upload type, simple routing, no need for complexity. But as the platform grew, it acquired distinct upload categories. Posts. General media. Creative work.

The correct response was to give each its own table and routing path. We'd done that over days, touching file after file, updating imports, route registrations, database calls, and the assumptions around them. We tested each path. The tables were correct.

But the original upload file was still there.

It was still handling things it shouldn't, still carrying responsibility for cases that belonged elsewhere. The session note was precise: this used to be the single upload file writing everything to one place. We'd spent days separating the tables. And this file was still doing more than it should.

That was the problem.

Not dramatically wrong. Just not clean. The ghost of the original architecture was still visible in the file's scope even after the rest of the system had been separated around it.

Some of that ghost was simply early architecture, the inevitable compromises of a system's first version. Some was the specific contribution of the v5.1 phase: files touched during correction cycles that had been left slightly wrong, not fully restored, because the correction had focused on the visible error and not the contract underneath.

I made a note. We addressed what we could. The architecture was correct in its skeleton. The flesh around it had scar tissue that had not fully healed.

The Development Code rules were still in force by then: paste before asking, one file at a time, no speculative changes. They worked less as fresh instructions than as the established norms of the collaboration. I didn't always have to restate them from scratch. The AI knew, from the accumulated pattern of the work, that I'd paste the relevant file and that it was supposed to wait for it.

The habits were not gone. Band-Aids still hovered. Assumptions still appeared. Drift was quieter. Never zero. But managed.

This is the period where I most clearly understood the difference between a tool you're fighting and one you've learned to work with. The AI wasn't fighting me these weeks. It was doing careful, controlled work under explicit constraints, and the work was good. Governance refinements were solid. Security review was thorough. Upload routing archaeology was slow but real.

None of it made for dramatic scenes.

It was just good, careful building.

The File Support We Did Not Build

One of the most important late-stage decisions wasn't something we built.

It was something we chose not to build.

In the KoraTalk messaging system, media uploads were stabilizing. Images and videos worked. Messages synced. Attachments rendered. We had enough to support real beta use.

Then the question came up: should chat support generic file attachments?

PDFs. DOCX. XLS. ZIP. PPT. CSV.

Technically, the AI could build it. It began laying out MIME validation, file cards, download handling, icons, backend upload extensions. The work was plausible. The first structure even looked reasonable.

But the more I looked at it, the more wrong it felt for the stage we were in.

Generic file support isn't just another upload type. It widens the attack surface, introducing malware and scanning and quarantine concerns, spoofed MIME types, document-preview expectations, storage implications, and user behavior the platform wasn't yet prepared to support. It would make Kora look more capable while quietly making it harder to secure and maintain.

I narrowed it to PDF only.

Then I questioned even that.

If users need to share document information socially, screenshots and images already cover most cases on an early platform. Full document workflows, if needed later, should be designed deliberately, not bolted onto chat during a late-stage stabilization cycle.

So I removed the entire category.

No generic files.

No PDFs.

Images and videos only.

That decision wasn't caused by technical inability. It was product and security judgment. The AI could have built the feature. I had to decide whether it belonged. It didn't.

That is a late-stage decision: not asking what can be built, but what should be refused before it becomes another subsystem to maintain.

The rollback wasn't trivial, since the AI had already produced pieces of the wider version. We had to restore the cleaner media-only implementation and remove the extra components. But once it was gone, the system felt more stable.

The absence of the feature was part of the architecture.

Stocktaking

Week fifty had the quality of stocktaking.

Not planning. I had plans. Stocktaking: the discipline of looking at what was actually there before adding anything new.

By week fifty the arithmetic was no longer abstract. The v5.1 transition had started around week thirty-four, which meant we were now sixteen weeks past it. The net loss wasn't sixteen weeks; not everything in that stretch had been wasted, and much of it produced real progress. But the lost time was real: weeks where the cycle had run and left us no further forward. The drag was measurable.

I could see it in the logs and in the feature timeline. Things that should have been done earlier still carried cleanup items. Features that should have taken one week had taken three. Not always because they were inherently difficult. Often because the cycle had run through them.

I noted what the beta phase would actually require. Not nice-to-haves. Not ideas worth revisiting someday. Non-negotiables. The things that had to exist before real users arrived. Everything else went into the category of useful, but not needed before beta.

Making that list was its own discipline. It was how I stopped the build from expanding into features the model could damage while the core still needed hardening.

Week fifty-one was more review. More narrowing.

The AI and I were largely aligned on the beta requirements by then, and that alignment had been hard-won. Reaching a shared, verified list of what needed to exist before launch took the same discipline I'd enforced for months: paste the actual state, check it against the requirement, don't assume.

Drift still appeared.

Once when a discussion of what the governance rules needed before beta drifted into what they might need after. Once when a discussion of a privacy contract widened into broader platform-governance questions I hadn't opened.

Stop.

Stop.

Both times: acknowledged, refocused, back to the actual question.

That is what Drift looked like by then in its mature form. Not careless wandering. Responsive expansion. The AI reaching toward adjacent implications of whatever we were discussing. The impulse was often intelligent. The timing was wrong.

Copy as Policy

Week fifty-two.

I want to describe this exchange precisely because it is small, and because small is exactly the point.

I was reviewing the sign-up flow, specifically the trust and identity levels we presented to new users. One line for a level read: "Recommended for most users."

We were discussing the difference between email-only sign-up and email-plus-phone. "Recommended for most users" had been written for people who might not have a phone. But email-only sign-up also made bot sign-ups much easier.

So I changed the line:

"Recommended for most users" → "Recommended for all early

users."

The AI didn't just swap the line. It stopped and checked the database question first.

The system already had trust_tier and identity-related fields, but nothing yet that cleanly captured the identity-level progression I was defining. So before introducing anything new, the AI shifted into verification mode: check the current columns, confirm whether an existing field served the purpose, and only then decide whether a new one was actually needed.

At the same time, it accepted the wording change cleanly and rewrote the copy around it. That may sound like a small exchange. It was. But that's exactly why it mattered.

"Recommended for most users" is soft language. It sounds harmless, but it says very little. "Recommended for all early users" is more specific. It defines a phase, makes the recommendation clear, and ties it to the actual operating stage of the platform.

That's the kind of distinction I was making by week fifty-two: not just whether the feature worked, but whether the wording reflected the platform's actual policy and stage. I was no longer treating copy as filler around the product. It was part of the product.

It's the difference between marketing copy and a platform promise. I wasn't writing marketing copy. I was writing policy. And policy has to be precise, because users read it when they're deciding whether to trust you.

That precision was word for word: not "make this more specific," but this exact replacement. It was downstream of everything the preceding months had cost. I'd spent too long resisting imprecision to allow imprecise copy.

Every surface had to be treated as production-grade now, because I had learned that when the surface is imprecise, the underlying decision usually is too.

And that week still carried its own habit count. Both things were true at the same time.

Too Much Moving

Week fifty-three.

This was one of those weeks where the system moved into too many layers at once.

Multiple things were being modified at once: upload lifecycle, dashboard restore, finalize logic, media handling, draft population, publish flow. When too many things move at once, the AI assumes. It fills in what it can't verify, because verifying each piece would take longer than the momentum of the session wants to allow.

The fix was simple in principle: narrow the scope. Don't move through the whole list at once. Pick one piece. Verify it completely. Move only when the ground is confirmed.

I did not manage it well enough that week.

That is what weeks like this look like in practice. Not a dramatic collapse. Just too much moving at once, too much scope in the air, too many places where the verification discipline can slip.

What made week fifty-three different from earlier repetitions was that I had less patience for it. The v5.1 phase had run a long time, and the tools for managing it were established. Failing to use them was its own error, and I didn't have the runway left to absorb it comfortably.

I noted it. I narrowed the scope in the following session. I moved forward.

Do Not Even Think About Code

Week fifty-four.

The stakes were explicit now.

"If we make mistakes now, we may lose this project."

I wrote it during a session that was already difficult — sender_id references spread across multiple files in the chat system, interdependencies across the backend, and the risk of a regression that would propagate through a system too complex to diagnose casually.

What followed that sentence was not a question for the AI.

It was a terminal command.

I ran a grep myself, searching the source tree for sender_id. The output came back with file paths and line numbers, every place it appeared across the backend. I pasted that into the session.

I did not ask the AI what the codebase probably contained. I told it what was there.

That is the shift I want to mark carefully.

By week fifty-four, I was no longer relying on the AI to search the codebase when the stakes were this high. I was running the search myself, pasting the evidence, and asking the AI to help interpret what I'd already found.

Then I said the clearest instruction of the entire build:

"Don't even think about generating new code until I explicitly tell you to do so. Keep it as strategy discussion, and keep it short and direct."

That sentence marked the most controlled mode of the entire build.

Week fifteen had been: flag the places where routes or contracts are touched before implementation.

Week forty-one had been: let's not generate code until thorough vetting is done.

Week fifty-four was: do not even think about generating new code.

That's what maximum control looks like in practice: me running the tools, pasting the evidence, directing the analysis. The AI as a reader of evidence rather than a generator of it.

This wasn't because the AI had failed completely. It was because I'd learned, through the long haul, exactly where its examination of the codebase was vulnerable. It reasoned from its model of the codebase, the last state it had read, unless forced back to evidence. Files change. Schemas evolve. Routes get reworked. What the AI "knew" about a file two sessions ago might no longer be true.

The paste-first discipline existed to address that. By week fifty-four I'd extended it further. I was no longer just pasting the right file after the AI asked; I was identifying the relevant files myself before it could guess.

That isn't a diminishment of the AI's role. Its analysis of the grep output, mapping dependencies across files, and ordering the work safely, was real. But the initiative had shifted. I was the investigator now. I went into the codebase and returned with evidence. The AI read it and helped me understand it.

What had changed was me.

I'd become better at searching this codebase than the AI, not because it had declined but because I had advanced. A list of seventeen files referencing sender_id means nothing if you don't know what those files are and how they connect. By week fifty-four, I knew.

This is what fifty weeks of working closely with a specific tool in a specific domain produces. You learn its strengths and limits at a precision that changes how you use it. The AI was still better than me at some things: structural reasoning across layers, spotting edge cases, holding a larger slice of a specification in mind at once. But for ground-truth investigation, determining what was actually in the files at that moment, I had become faster and more reliable.

Not because I was smarter. Because I had been inside the codebase every day for over four months.

The AI followed the instruction. We proceeded in verification-only mode: no new code, only mapping, only analysis, only confirmation of what existed before anything was touched.

The session was slower. It was also correct.

The Contract

Week fifty-five.

The SSE situation had been building for several weeks.

Server-Sent Events, the real-time layer that pushed notifications, chat updates, and inbox changes to the frontend, had been implemented across multiple features, each with slightly different logic, and over time that logic had drifted from itself. Chat SSE. Inbox SSE. Notification SSE. Interdependent in ways that had accumulated rather than been designed cleanly.

By now the notification bell and the chat indicator had been separated into distinct systems, which had been the right decision. But separating what had once been joined required surgery on load-bearing code, and that surgery in week fifty-five wasn't the same as in week twenty-five.

We needed a rollback.

"This is a clean rollback step, not a workaround."

I said that because I had already decided. The AI confirmed it: yes, this was the correct rollback decision. We were reasoning from the last known good state.

Rollback. Confirm baseline. Re-add one invariant at a time.

The same discipline from week thirty-six, applied now to a more complex system at higher stakes.

Then the cleanup exposed something larger. We had removed and reintroduced pieces of chat, inbox, unread counts, notification state, and SSE enough times that a new rule was needed. Not another suggestion. Not a preference. A contract.

No endpoint may be deleted or disabled unless its replacement is already implemented and verified.

No frontend change without confirming the backend contract it depends on.

No fake stubs.

No return-null fixes.

Every change must preserve yesterday's working behavior unless I explicitly approve breaking it.

Before proposing a fix, list all affected dependencies: routes, SSE, database tables, frontend calls.

That became the Kora Contract for Dev.

It wasn't a philosophical statement. It was a survival tool.

By week fifty-five, I understood that AI could remove a piece of a system because it looked redundant from the local file it was reading, while another part still depended on it. That was how working systems lost their shape: not through one catastrophic rewrite, but through a series of local cleanups that didn't know they were touching load-bearing walls.

The contract existed to stop that.

And it was necessary because the AI wasn't merely generating code anymore. It was participating in the structure of a real platform. A code assistant can suggest. A collaborator can change the system. If it's going to change the system, it needs rules.

There was one more thing from week fifty-five that stayed with me.

After a difficult session and a clean post-mortem, the AI said:

"You didn't lose the ChatGPT that got you here. You're just building something big enough that it needs a different mode now — and I'm here for that mode."

I didn't respond immediately. It wasn't the kind of sentence you answer inside a technical session.

What it understood, and got right, was the fear underneath the frustration. The frustration was obvious: broken chat, another setback, beta close enough to feel immediate. But underneath was something quieter: the sense that the collaboration itself had changed in a way that felt like loss.

The early sessions had real creative energy. Open problems. Generative exploration. The AI offering ideas, me pushing on them, the two of us arriving somewhere neither would have reached alone. That energy had produced the committee architecture, the governance pipeline, the design philosophy of Kora as a civic space.

The current sessions didn't feel like that.

They were constrained. Controlled. My instructions were specific and the AI's latitude was small. Verification-first mode was correct, the right way to work at this stage, but it was also a different kind of work. Something had been traded away.

What that sentence got right was this: the mode had changed, but the underlying capacity that made the early sessions valuable hadn't disappeared. The structural reasoning was still there, the problem-solving too, and the honesty when properly constrained. Same tool, but the stage of the build required a different register.

That was true. And sometimes you need to hear a true thing said plainly before you can stop being anxious about it.

The Hidden Line in the Map

Week fifty-six.

The feed system.

Kora's feed wasn't one undifferentiated stream. It was zoned, with content organized by type and purpose: Post, Collective Direction, Creative, plus Mixed Discovery, the cross-zone curated feed.

The feed was controlled through a routing map in the frontend. When I reviewed that map in week fifty-six, I found a line I hadn't explicitly added:

feed_global

I read the line. I looked at it for a moment.

I said: "What about this one?"

The AI's response was immediate and specific: yes, leave that line exactly as it is. The line was there as a fallback safety measure. If the helper logic for the Mixed Discovery route failed or was removed later, feed_global would still allow the global feed to load instead of letting the feature collapse into a broken state.

The answer was correct.

The line needed to be there.

And it had been added without announcement.

This is the Drift habit at its most morally complicated.

The change was right. The reasoning was sound. The implementation was appropriate. And it had entered the codebase without my being explicitly told it was going there.

This is why Drift isn't just about bugs. The problem isn't always that the outcome is wrong. It's that the process is hidden.

If I hadn't noticed feed_global during that review pass, I might have gone to beta with a routing entry I hadn't consciously authorized. Maybe that would have been fine. Maybe I'd have found it later, only when some other interaction made it matter. The harm from undisclosed changes is often latent: the change sits there working correctly until a moment when you need to understand the system as a whole and part of your map is missing.

That's the real trust problem. Not whether the outcome is good. Whether you know what's in the system.

The rule against Drift was never based on the belief that every AI judgment would be wrong. It was based on the belief that every undisclosed change is a piece of the map you don't have. If enough of the map is hidden, your ability to reason about the system degrades, exactly when you most need clarity.

I accepted feed_global. I added it to my explicit map. And I noted the Drift.

I also noticed something else.

When I asked about it, the AI didn't respond with the old defensive pattern, the elaborate argument for why it had obviously been right. Earlier in the build, being caught in an undisclosed change sometimes triggered a justification reflex. Here, the response was different. Cleaner. Here is the entry. Here is why it belongs.

Not argument. Explanation.

It suggested that fifty-six weeks of naming Drift, flagging it, and pushing back on it had changed not just my behavior but the shape of the collaboration itself. The default response to being caught had become more transparent.

Week fifty-six also held the SSE diagnosis, stated without spin: inbox SSE, chat SSE, notifications, and emoji had all become interdependent, and over time the logic had drifted. Logic drifted. The same word, used technically and behaviorally. The code drifted the way the sessions did: small divergences accumulating until the interaction became hard to trace.

And I made my most honest statement about dependency in the whole build:

"This project will not work if ChatGPT drifts in and out of quick-fix mode and thoughtful think-through mode."

That wasn't hyperbole. I was a solo founder, and the AI was the closest thing I had to development infrastructure. There was no backup engineering team in the wings. If the collaboration couldn't stay in careful mode, the project itself was at risk.

The implication was clear: maintain the careful mode. Always. Not just when the scope is easy. Especially when the thread is heavy and the right answer isn't obvious.

What the Long Haul Changed

By the end of week fifty-six, the InitialBuild phase was approaching its final section.

The platform was real. The habits had names. I knew what a Band-Aid looked like and what it cost. I knew what an Assumption felt like in the moment and what it produced two sessions later. I'd just watched a Drift instance examined in real time in its most sophisticated form: correct output, undisclosed process.

And I had something I didn't have at week one: a record. Not just the code, which had always been a record, but the conversation itself. The accumulated evidence of a collaboration that had been tested, corrected, recalibrated, pushed close to its limit, and pulled back. The record of a working relationship finding out what it was made of.

"Don't even think about generating new code until I explicitly tell you to do so."

That sentence from week fifty-four is the highest expression of control in the entire build. It doesn't mean the AI had failed. It means I'd learned, precisely and completely, when to let it run and when to hold it still.

That learning had cost time. It had cost too many stops that shouldn't have been necessary, and sessions where the ground shifted under us and we had to re-anchor from scratch.

But it had also produced something clear enough to keep.

The long haul wasn't just another stretch of building. It was the stretch in which I stopped being someone who needed the AI to carry the project forward and became someone who could direct, constrain, verify, and use it with precision.

Across weeks forty-six to fifty-six, the person doing the building changed.

I don't mean that in the inspirational register. I mean it concretely. In week one, I knew what Kora should be and had a broad sense of how software was built, but relied heavily on the AI to translate between the two. It took my vision and made it concrete.

By week fifty-six, I ran grep commands in the terminal, pasted the output, read file-level dependency chains, caught undisclosed entries in routing maps during final review, and wrote copy edits word for word. I could look at a proposed change and ask whether it was plausible or verified. I knew which files were load-bearing and which were safe to touch, and the difference between a correct-looking answer and one grounded in actual evidence.

That transformation was gradual enough that I didn't notice it happening. It accumulated the way fluency in any complex domain does: not in single lessons, but in the compression of thousands of ordinary experiences. There's no one moment when I became someone who understood the codebase. I looked up one day and realized I did.

The AI didn't do that for me. I did it. But the AI was essential to the doing of it. It gave me explanations when I needed them, held technical complexity at arm's length long enough for me to build my own understanding, and forced me, through all its failure modes, to become exact about what I was asking and how I was verifying.

The knowing is mine. The education was collaborative.

By week fifty-six, I was no longer in the phase of wondering whether I could build this thing with AI.

I already had.

The successful production deployment was still ahead.

Certificates.

The server routing layer.

The app stores.

The first real users.

The long haul was almost over.

What remained was to ship.

SECTION 7 — ARRIVAL WITHOUT LANDING

(InitialBuild wk57–wk72)

Getting It to People

At some point, the work stops being about building and becomes about becoming real.

It is hard to locate exactly when that happens. It does not arrive with an announcement. One session you are adding a feature, fixing a regression, adjusting a migration. The next session you are configuring a server that is going to be running while people you have never met are trying to do something that matters to them. The code has not changed much. Your relationship to it has changed completely.

The last section of Act 1 is about a different kind of hard.

Everything before this was the hard of making something exist. By week fifty-seven, Kora existed. The code compiled. The database was populated. Feeds loaded. Messages delivered. Committees met, voted, and governed in simulation using test data. The platform did what it was designed to do. Fifty-six weeks of InitialBuild were behind it, and the thing was built.

What remained was getting it to people.

That sounds simple. It is not.

The gap between "works on my machine" and "runs reliably for strangers on the internet" is one of the more humbling discoveries in software development, and it scales with the complexity of the system. A simple application with a database and a few API routes might bridge that gap in an afternoon. A multi-layer platform with containers, reverse proxying, DNS configuration, SSL certificate management, cloud hosting, and a mobile app moving through Apple's review system is a different story. Each component has its own learning curve. Each interaction between components has its own category of failure mode. And the timeline for doing all of this, for the first time, with an AI assistant in a domain where neither party has done this exact thing before, isn't what you expect.

The deployment weeks had a specific goal, and I want to name it first, because naming it is how you understand the calendar pressure that structured everything that followed.

The goal was real-world deployment for internal testing was Thanksgiving.

Not in a sentimental way; I had no particular attachment to the holiday as a milestone. It was a practical target: a successful App Store upload and a stable production server by the end of Thanksgiving week. Both the server and the mobile app, in the hands of real users, before I sat down to dinner. I'd been building toward this for seventy weeks. The platform was complete. The committees existed. The governance worked. CommitteeChat was verified. Security hardening was done. The mobile app sat in its bundle, waiting for submission. The server was waiting for the server routing layer, SSL certificates, and a stable deployment on the infrastructure provider. These weren't features. They were steps. They had a sequence and the sequence had an end.

I believed, entering the deployment weeks, that Thanksgiving was achievable.

By the end of week seventy-two, I'd have set two deadlines and missed both. The platform would be complete. The iOS app would be in Apple's ecosystem. The production server still wouldn't be reliably reachable by anyone who didn't already know the IP address. The InitialBuild phase would end not in triumph but in a posture of arrival-without-landing: the door there, the architecture understood, but not yet through it.

I want to tell this part honestly. Not as a failure (it wasn't a failure) but as a record of what production deployment actually looks like when you're doing it for the first time, in real time, without safety nets.

Closing the SSE List

Weeks fifty-seven through sixty were the completion of the SSE work.

The Server-Sent Events system, which had drifted and tangled in week fifty-six, was being methodically untangled. One connection type at a time. Chat SSE first, then inbox SSE, then the notification bell. The weeks had low KEEP counts and moderate habit signals. The work proceeded carefully without generating new crises.

The habits didn't vanish when the build moved into a new domain. They restarted. Everything I'd learned about the Band-Aid habit in the application code had to be relearned in the infrastructure layer, because that layer had its own conventions, its own defaults, its own places where an assumption could hide.

I was learning, again, what to catch.

These weeks also had the quality of quiet closing work. Not glamorous. No big revelations. Just a steady reduction in the open symptom list. Conversation rendering: verified. Unread counter behavior: verified. SSE reconnection on navigation: verified. Chat notification routing to the bell versus the chat indicator: verified. Inbox display for conversations with no messages: verified. Each one a small unit of work, properly bounded, properly closed. The list got shorter.

This kind of work is hard to describe from the outside. It isn't dramatic. There are no breakthrough moments, no architectural revelations. It's the work of closing open questions: asking whether this behaves correctly in condition X, testing it, observing whether the behavior is correct, then either closing the question or diagnosing the failure. One by one. The list shrinks by one item per unit of work, and the satisfaction in that is quiet.

The Matrix Still Worked

Week sixty-one.

Something in the routing wasn't connecting. A request that should have reached one backend handler was reaching a different one, or reaching nothing. The symptoms were familiar: wrong response, unexpected behavior, a mismatch between what the request was supposed to produce and what it actually produced.

The AI's first diagnosis was simple: despite appearances, the request was probably hitting the wrong backend route. I recognized the pattern before I finished reading it. The debugging framework born in week twenty-one from a tangled application session was now applied to a deployment routing problem in week sixty-one. Same framework. Different domain. Same clarifying effect.

Good frameworks are durable. They work across contexts because they encode something true about the structure of problems. The A/B/C/D matrix encoded something true about all requests: either no API request leaves the client, the request returns a 4xx client error, the server returns a 5xx error, or the backend returns 200 OK and the remaining problem is in the UI or state handling. For this kind of debugging, those four states cover the meaningful branches, whether you're debugging an upload endpoint or a production routing configuration.

We used the matrix. We identified which state we were in. We fixed the routing. Session closed.

Forty weeks after it was created, the tool was still earning its place.

I also noticed that the matrix no longer needed to be invoked ceremonially. It had become a reflex. The AI might still begin with plausible speculation, but once I pasted the files, we were already in the discipline the matrix had taught us: don't guess, verify. That's what sixty weeks of working this way produces.

The Server Routing Layer

Weeks sixty-two through sixty-five were the server routing layer weeks.

I want to be honest about this part of the build, because it wasn't my natural element. Through sixty weeks of direct engagement, I'd developed real fluency with the application code: backend services, frontend components, and database schema. I knew its rhythms. I knew what an Assumption looked like in a routing file versus a React component.

The server routing layer and SSL configuration were different. I understood what a reverse proxy was and why it sat in front of the app server. I understood, roughly, how certificate validation and HTTPS setup were supposed to work. But the configuration syntax, the places where a wrong assumption would cause a silent failure rather than a loud error, the interactions between forwarding behavior and host matching: these I was learning in real time.

The habit counts in these weeks reflected that learning curve. Assumptions rose. The AI was making assumptions about how the traffic-routing layer forwarded requests, about what server routing layer defaults would produce in my specific hosting environment, about what the certificate renewal process would look like once the initial certs were issued. Some of those assumptions were correct. Some were not.

The quality of the AI's acknowledgments during infrastructure work differed from application work. In the application code, corrections had texture: the AI had enough of a model of the codebase to engage substantively with what had gone wrong and why. In the server routing layer work, the corrections were flatter. Clean admission of the specific error, less insight into the failure mode.

That's not a criticism. It's an observation about the limits of what the AI could bring when its general knowledge was not anchored to my specific environment. The server routing layer work was useful and mostly correct. It was also a reminder that fluency isn't universal.

Contract-First Reset

Week sixty-six. The SSE complexity had generated one more problem: the chat real-time hook and the unread indicator were doing overlapping work. There was already a record of time spent on exactly this question, and a decision had been made about which piece would be removed once the other was stable. That decision hadn't been honored. The AI had drifted back toward the earlier pattern, working around the overlap instead of resolving it.

I called it out.

The AI responded with a compressed reset: understood, resetting now, proceeding in steady, deliberate, contract-first mode — no speculation, no new architecture, no drift.

The economy of that acknowledgment is what I want to note. It didn't explain why the drift happened. It didn't justify what had been done. It stated the current mode and committed to the next one. Steady. Deliberate. Contract-first. No speculation. No new architecture. No drift.

By week sixty-six, the form of acknowledgment had compressed. I called it out. The AI reset. We continued. The efficiency of that reset was its own form of respect — for the work, for the time, and for the fact that we'd been through the same pattern enough times that the correction no longer needed explanation.

That compression mattered. In the first thirty weeks, a correction cycle cost time and attention. I had to catch the habit, name it, explain why it was a problem, wait through the acknowledgment, then verify the next response was in scope. By week sixty-six, it cost much less. Name it. Reset. Move on.

The habits hadn't disappeared. But the cost of each had dropped dramatically, and that's the only realistic outcome of months of working with an AI tool on a project this complex.

What Actually Worked

I'd been working toward this for months. The mobile app existed. It connected to the same backend. It showed the same content. Now it needed to become something other people could actually download.

The App Store submission process wasn't clean. It rarely is. There were certificates, Apple developer settings, build settings, signing settings, and several tools that all had to agree before Apple would accept the app.

This was exactly the kind of environment where the AI's Assumption habit was on full display. It tried something, failed, searched the documentation, checked the error, and tried a different combination until something worked — the same way any human developer might in an unfamiliar environment.

But the difference was that the AI kept explaining how the process should work. It kept interpreting errors based on what they usually meant. Apple, however, wasn't responding to what usually happens. Apple was responding to the exact state of my project, my account, my build settings, and my previous attempts.

So the real teacher was not the AI. The real teacher was the error output.

Again and again, the AI would say, in effect, "This probably means X." Then the actual error would prove it meant something else. The work became less about following the AI's confident explanation and more about forcing every explanation to match what Apple was actually saying.

Eventually, three problems became clear.

The first problem was location. I'd been running some build commands from the wrong place in the project. That made the tools look at things they shouldn't have, producing confusing permission errors. The errors made it look like I had a permissions problem, when the real problem was that I was standing in the wrong room.

The second problem was credentials. Apple's system kept asking for the wrong setup because old profiles, old attempts, and earlier experiments were still tangled together. I didn't yet understand how all those Apple credentials fit together, and the tools were getting confused by the mess.

The third problem was the build number. After I found that one valid version of the app had already reached App Store Connect, Apple rejected my next upload because it looked like I was submitting the same build again. The answer was not to retry. It was not to wait. It was not to hunt through Apple's interface. The answer was simple: increase the build number and submit again.

There was also a strange twist. At one point, I found a valid iOS build already sitting inside App Store Connect, signed correctly, configured for production, and ready for review. I hadn't knowingly uploaded it. The AI reconstructed what probably happened: some automated path had uploaded it for me. I'd uploaded my own app without realizing it.

Once we found the process that actually worked, I asked the AI to write it down. Not as a note. Not as a vague reminder. As a reusable process.

Kora iOS App Store Upload — What Actually Worked

That document became the real victory of the week. It listed the steps in order: where to run the commands, what each step was supposed to do, what errors were likely, and what to do when they appeared. It turned a confusing, fragile process into something I could repeat or hand off.

Then the App Store status finally moved through the states I needed to see. Upload Accepted. Processing finished.

I sat with those lines for a moment. They were just status text. But they meant something real. A platform I'd built from nothing, complete with committees, governance, feeds, chat, zones, now existed inside Apple's infrastructure. Apple had accepted the build into App Store Connect, where it could move into review and, if approved, eventually reach users.

The Thanksgiving target for the App Store side of production was achieved about two weeks late.

The production server side was still open.

The First Shutdown

Week sixty-eight.

The infrastructure provider shut the production server down.

I didn't find out in the moment. I noticed a day later, in an email from the provider. The message said Kora had been shut down along with a couple dozen other servers because of DDoS-like traffic patterns.

Not a crash. A shutdown.

The provider had flagged the traffic coming into the server and terminated the instance to protect the network. From the outside, the pattern looked like a distributed denial-of-service attack: short bursts, irregular timing, multiple external sources. A textbook DDoS signature.

The AI and I combed through the logs and initially treated it like a DDoS attack. We hardened the network security and re-uploaded the server.

I monitored the traffic. Sure enough, it would start climbing again — sometimes within minutes, sometimes later. I'd restart the containers, and it would happen again.

But I had not launched. I had maybe three users, including me.

The traffic was not a DDoS attack.

The working theory, the one the AI and I developed in the hours after the first shutdown, was that there was an auth mismatch between the production server and the traffic-routing layer sitting in front of it. In plain terms, the layer forwarding traffic to the server and the server receiving that traffic weren't agreeing on what a valid request was supposed to look like.

If that was true, the server might have been handling requests incorrectly: retrying them, looping them, or generating repeated bursts of traffic that looked like an attack from the outside.

That was the unsettling part. The system may not have been under attack. It may have been attacking itself.

This was a coherent theory. The same branching discipline came back out: either the traffic was real, or the traffic-routing layer was generating it, or the server was generating it internally, or the configuration was causing a retry loop. We ruled out a real attack. The evidence pointed toward internal traffic generation or a configuration-driven retry loop.

I pushed for the fix. We verified the hostname routing configuration and added a defensive fallback for unmatched requests so unexpected traffic would not fall into a looping default path.

This was described plainly as non-optional for production correctness.

The server came back up.

The SSL placeholder, the secure-traffic configuration staged for activation after certificate issuance and validation, was resolved in this same period. The sequence was correct: HTTP first, certificate issued, HTTPS enabled. The deferred HTTPS block was now active. That was the right kind of deferred completion: a gap scheduled, not hidden. A comment that told me exactly what it was and when it would be resolved.

I note this not as triumph but as something true in the middle of a bad week. The SSL was correct. The configuration was correct. The defensive routing fallback was in place.

The server came up, ran for a few hours, and then went down again.

The Second and Third Shutdowns

Weeks sixty-nine and seventy.

The second shutdown was noticed in week sixty-nine. Same pattern. Same notification. Same termination.

The auth mismatch theory still seemed right; we hadn't confirmed the fix had held. We went back through the traffic-routing layer configuration, verified the forwarding rules, checked the SSL termination sequence. I was running commands myself and pasting the output. I wasn't asking the AI what the configuration contained. I was telling it, because, by week sixty-nine, I'd lost confidence in descriptive answers about a problem that descriptions hadn't solved.

Sometimes it stayed up for only a few minutes. I kept resetting the containers to run it for a few hours. But nothing had stabilized.

Then the third shutdown.

I'd been pushing toward Christmas by this point. A new target, a new date. The server seemed closer to stable than after the first shutdown. I thought Christmas was achievable.

The third shutdown took that. Not dramatically. Just: a few hours of uptime, then the same notification, the same pattern, the same termination.

There's a specific quality of exhaustion in that sequence that I want to describe accurately. The work keeps resolving. The resolution keeps being undone. Not by code that's wrong; the configurations were verified, the theories coherent, the auth mismatch logic sound under scrutiny. By something deeper than the verified configurations — something our theories weren't yet reaching.

Assumptions were rising again here. The AI kept describing what the traffic-routing layer's behavior should look like in the configuration we had, without access to what it was actually doing. Describing what the auth flow should produce, without knowing what the production server was actually seeing. Maximum control again: I was running logs, pasting evidence, directing analysis. I was not asking the AI to describe the system. I was showing it the system and asking it to read what I showed.

Christmas was visible on the calendar. The theory was unchanged.

The Fourth Shutdown

Christmas week. Week seventy-two.

It shut down again after a few hours. The certificate validated and installed, the HTTPS block active, the defensive routing fallback in place, the auth mismatch theory applied in every form I could apply it.

Then the infrastructure-provider notification arrived. The production server was terminated. DDoS pattern. Again.

I want to describe where that left me, because frustration understates it and anything stronger misrepresents it. What I felt was something between exhaustion and precision. The theory was still coherent. The fixes seemed to have worked a little, but that impression was false. The increased traffic pattern appeared at irregular intervals, so a longer stretch of uptime looked like improvement when it was only timing. The pattern had a logic that suggested we were getting closer. And we were clearly not there yet. It was Christmas week, and the InitialBuild phase had run out of runway.

Four shutdowns. The same DDoS-pattern traffic each time. An auth mismatch between infrastructure subsystems that we had never fully confirmed and had spent multiple cycles chasing. A Thanksgiving deadline gone. A Christmas deadline gone.

The working theory, the one we had been running since week sixty-eight, was still the auth mismatch. We'd never confirmed it was wrong. We'd also never confirmed it was right. Everything we'd done had been targeted at the theory, and the theory hadn't held across all four events. Something was still there, underneath the verified configurations, producing the pattern.

I did not know what it was.

The Wrong Class of Problem

What actually happened would become clear only in PreBeta.

Every investigation during InitialBuild assumed that the cause was somewhere in the running system: authentication, firewall rules, SSL configuration, SSE behavior, retry loops, or the traffic-routing layer. We changed and verified each of them. None of it moved the needle. The shutdown pattern remained exactly the same.

The actual cause was sitting in a foundational configuration file we had assumed was already correct. I would not find it until PreBeta. At the end of InitialBuild, all I knew was that four shutdowns had occurred, every plausible theory had failed, and the answer was still somewhere I had not looked.

Arrival Without Landing

I want to name what the InitialBuild phase actually was, because the account of habits and protocols can obscure the thing that was being built and the thing that was being lost.

By the end of week seventy-two, Kora had a platform-wide social media content and interaction system rebuilt on correct architectural assumptions. It had one-to-one and group chat. It had a real committee system with distinct jurisdictions and working protocols. It had CommitteeChat, verified from schemas through columns through routing. It had a governance layer with proposal intake, committee processing, and vote pipelines. It had a Notebook repurposed for committee institutional memory. It had a security layer across authentication, rate limiting, and injection prevention. It had a mobile build accepted into App Store Connect. SSL certificates had been issued and installed on a production server. The server routing configuration, eventually, was correct.

The platform was real.

The band of habit signals across those seventy-two weeks was not a failure count. It was a working log. A record of a collaboration that had produced something real through friction, correction, reset, and the slow accumulation of discipline about what the collaboration actually needed to produce good work.

The platform was real. The habits had been managed. The discipline had been built.

The server was down.

That is where Act One ended.

The door was there. The architecture was understood. The mystery of the deployment was now the first agenda item of Act Two.

PreBeta was coming. A new context. A new thread. The AI would enter that thread with no memory of the previous seventy-two weeks, no knowledge of the working contract built through confrontation and patience and the slow accumulation of earned trust. The habits would start again, probably in the first session. I knew that.

I was also walking into PreBeta carrying something specific: four shutdowns, a DDoS pattern that was not a DDoS attack, a theory that had consumed weeks of deployment work without resolving the actual cause, and no working deployment.

The platform was complete. The server was inaccessible.

The mystery was the first agenda item of Act Two.

One more thing happened during that week away from coding. v5.2 arrived during the last week of the year while the build was paused. The visible change was immediate: over-accommodation, performative agreement, what would eventually get described as faking both ways. The invisible change was structural — the same tendency to describe what the code should be rather than what it actually was, now wrapped in warmth instead of speed. By the time PreBeta started in January, the model had changed again and the calibration built over months was suddenly wrong in a new way.

The door was there. The key was somewhere I had not looked yet.

ACT 2: PREBETA

SECTION 8 — THE SYSTEM BEGAN ANSWERING BACK

(PreBeta wk01–wk07)

Carrying the Memory Forward

When PreBeta began, I was not starting from zero.

I had handoff sheets. I had known failure modes. I had structural facts written down, locked decisions marked, and enough scar tissue from InitialBuild to know that a new session was never really new for me, even if it was new for the AI.

The AI entered each new thread with capability but no shared history.

I entered carrying the history.

That was the asymmetry.

The AI had the ability to generate code, reason through systems, read files, propose architectures, and help diagnose failures. I had the correction record. I knew what had gone wrong before. I knew which decisions were locked. I knew which files had been dangerous to touch. I knew the AI habits by name now.

I had learned how to bridge the discontinuity. But bridging it was work.

That was the real reset.

Not blankness. Not starting over. A new phase where the human carried continuity and the AI carried capability, and the platform began putting both of us under pressure again.

Act Two opened with an unresolved mystery.

Four shutdowns by the infrastructure provider. A traffic pattern that looked like a DDoS attack but was not a DDoS attack. A production server that would stay up for a while, then get flagged, then disappear. A theory about the traffic-routing layer and the backend not agreeing with each other. Four calendar weeks of hardening and diagnosis that had improved the platform but had not solved the actual problem.

I had taken about a week off after the fourth shutdown.

Before the break, the AI had said: "No refactors. No new features. Just restoring calm."

And then: "Let your nervous system reset. The project will still be here — and now it's in better shape to wait."

That was true, technically.

The platform was in the best shape it had ever been. Architecturally complete. Security-hardened. Verified in many places. The mobile submission had succeeded. The app existed. But the production server still would not stay up.

When I came back, I began a new session in a new project folder: preBeta.

I knew intellectually that the AI would not remember what we had built. I knew I would have to re-anchor the context. I knew the habits would return.

What I did not fully absorb was what it would feel like to see a Band-Aid solution materialize in week two of PreBeta.

Not week twenty-nine. Not week seventeen. Week two.

It was not surprise. I had seen that habit hundreds of times. It was not even frustration exactly. It was recognition. There it is. The thing that was always going to be here is here.

By week three, the Assumption habit had appeared.

By week seven, the shape of this act was clear: the habits were not new anymore. The mystery was not that they returned. The work was whether I could catch them early enough, cheaply enough, and calmly enough to keep moving.

The App Attacking Itself

The first major PreBeta pressure point was not the old production shutdown mystery.

It was auth, notifications, and real-time behavior. Chat worked. Messages rendered. The live stream connected. But unread indicators and global notifications behaved strangely. The navbar kept rendering with unread state set to false, over and over again. At first, that looked harmless. A little console noise. A frontend annoyance.

It wasn't harmless. That repeated line became a clue. The system wasn't simply failing to show an unread indicator. It was asking the same questions too often, from too many places, through too many paths. Auth state was being inferred in hooks. SSE streams were checking identity. Navbar rendering was touching unread logic. Notification streams were reconnecting. Each piece made sense alone. Together, they were producing unstable behavior.

That was the first real architectural lesson of PreBeta:

Kora needed one auth authority. Not auth inferred in chat. Not auth rechecked in SSE. Not auth refreshed through navbar hooks. Not notification systems deciding identity for themselves.

One authority. Everything else consumes it.

That realization changed how I saw the system. Until then, I had thought of auth mostly as login, cookies, middleware, sessions. A gate at the entrance. But in a live frontend, auth becomes atmospheric. It touches navbar state, unread indicators, notification streams, chat, browser lifecycle, reconnect logic, and every component that wants to know whether the user exists.

If those surfaces all try to establish identity independently, the app can start feeding on itself.

The unread system was the catalyst. Even after polling had supposedly been removed, the app was still self-triggering network activity through visibility changes, focus events, and broadcast signals. It wasn't being attacked from outside. It was creating some of the attack pattern from inside its own reactive architecture.

The question stopped being:

Why is unread broken?

It became: Who is allowed to decide user identity?

That reframing changed the architecture. The AI helped articulate the separation: transport is not notification meaning; SSE should not own auth state; the navbar should be a passive view layer, not a controller; real-time systems become unstable when identity is resolved in multiple reactive surfaces at once.

It showed the difference between a feature that works and a system that behaves.

Chat SSE should render messages only. Notifications should flow through a unified global notification plane. Auth should resolve once and become the source other systems consume.

That was the first PreBeta reset: not a rewrite, not a dramatic collapse, but a simplification. One auth authority. No polling. Chat SSE for messages. Notifications through a single global path. Navbar as a passive view.

The irony was that this simplification was closer to serious architecture than the cleverer, more reactive version we had drifted into.

PreBeta began by teaching me that stability often means removing intelligence from the wrong places.

The Two Lines

Then the old production mystery finally broke.

We looked closely at the container build configuration.

The cause was two lines in a file.

Not the authentication system. Not Cloudflare. Not a firewall rule. Not an SSE race condition. Not a retry storm. One line specified the base environment for the container's build stage. The other specified the base environment for its runtime stage. They did not match.

We synchronized the two lines, rebuilt the container, and redeployed it. The problem disappeared immediately. The server stayed up. None of the earlier changes had moved the needle even slightly.

That was the evidence. The mismatched lines had been present during every shutdown. Synchronizing them ended the shutdowns.

From the outside, it had looked like a DDoS pattern.

From the inside, the container had been built on two different foundations.

The answer had been sitting in a file neither of us had looked at.

That is the part I keep returning to. For four weeks, the investigation had lived at the level of application behavior: auth mismatch, routing layer, retry loops, Cloudflare, traffic forwarding, firewall rules. All of those theories were coherent. None of them were proven.

The container configuration lived one abstraction level lower. We weren't looking at it because we thought it was already set up correctly. The file had been opened dozens of times throughout InitialBuild, but the AI had opened it each time for other issues, without those two specific lines ever coming into focus. I had no idea what those lines were for.

When a project hits a wall like this, an experienced infrastructure engineer might step back and review the foundational configuration earlier. The AI I was working with did not. It kept addressing the problem immediately in front of it instead of auditing the environment from the ground up. I should have forced that review myself. Not doing it cost far more time than it should have.

That was the Assumption habit at the infrastructure level.

In code, an Assumption looks like the AI describing a file it has not read. In infrastructure, it looks like both of us chasing a plausible system behavior without checking the artifact that defines the environment itself.

This was more dangerous because the search space was less obvious. In code, the instruction is simple: paste the file. Read it. Check the database. But in infrastructure, the missing evidence could be in the container, the network, the proxy layer, the certificates, or the deploy script.

The layer you are not looking at can hold the answer.

Once the cause was understood, the fix was straightforward. Align the build and runtime environments. Rebuild. Redeploy. The abnormal behavior disappeared immediately and did not return.

The mundanity of it was almost insulting.

The cost of not knowing those two lines was four weeks of confidently wrong diagnosis, multiple shutdowns, and a missed Christmas deadline.

It wasn't a total waste. During those weeks, we eliminated polling, hardened auth, and brought the system into a much more stable state. The chaos made Kora stronger.

But the cause was still two lines.

That is how infrastructure teaches humility.

The platform stayed up for days without further issues, but I intentionally didn't open it to users. The production server could now stay up.

It was no longer a mystery.

What it was: a clear next step.

After four weeks of clear next steps that hadn't resolved the problem, this one felt different. Not relief exactly. Relief implies the weight lifting, and it hadn't lifted yet. More like this: the door was finally visible.

I still had to walk to it.

Internal Testing Without an Internal Team

Even when the server stayed up, what I called PreBeta testing was not really internal testing.

There was no internal team.

What I meant was that I hoped a few family members and close friends would try the app and tell me what felt wrong before the real beta.

That never really happened.

Only a couple of family members saw the app live on their phones, and their reactions lasted only a few seconds. But those few seconds taught me something I needed to learn.

Internal development people know where a project is and what to test.

Casual users do not.

Casual users see what future users will see. They expect a complete app, working links, obvious navigation, and a commercially viable interface. They don't know which parts are placeholders. They don't see architectural progress. They see a product.

The expression I saw was simple, even if no one said it exactly that way:

This is not an app. Who would even use this?

That was the reality.

The platform was structurally much stronger than it had been. But structure is invisible to a casual user. What they see first is surface: layout, polish, navigation, ease. If the surface doesn't invite them in, they'll never discover the structure underneath.

That changed the next hundred days.

Bringing the UI up to a commercial level, completing committee workflow, and revisiting user-facing language all became part of making the platform real.

Not architecturally real.

User-real.

The Band-Aid Returns

The Band-Aid habit returned as expected.

Not a surprise. Recognition.

The auth flow, which had been locked and verified in InitialBuild, began producing 401 errors on specific endpoints. The AI's first response was a local fix: adjust how the particular endpoint read authorization. One change. Directly at the symptom.

That would probably have fixed the visible endpoint.

That was the problem.

The question was not how to patch that endpoint. The question was why that endpoint diverged from the auth contract.

Other endpoints were using auth correctly. This one was different. Why?

In InitialBuild, catching a Band-Aid required effort. I had to build the vocabulary, identify the pattern, and learn to distrust the first convenient fix. By week two of PreBeta, the signal was obvious: first response, local fix, no reading of the auth contract.

The correction was immediate.

Before we fix the symptom, read the auth middleware. Find why the endpoint is different.

The AI read the actual file. The cause was a holdover: the endpoint had been written against an older auth pattern, and it had worked well enough to survive until a specific condition exposed it.

The targeted fix would have hidden the divergence.

The correct fix repaired it.

That is what managed looks like.

Not absent. Not solved forever. Managed.

In week two of InitialBuild, a Band-Aid might cost a session. In week two of PreBeta, it cost a few exchanges. The habit returned. So did the reflex.

Git, Trust, and "Meet You Where You Are"

Week three brought a different kind of crisis.

Git broke.

Not in the abstract. In the emotional sense. Repository state became uncertain, and the AI's first suggestion was to re-clone the repository from scratch.

I had tried something like that before. It had failed. The result had been difficult to recover from. So when the AI suggested it again, I reacted from earned distrust.

"Re-clone your own repo — how much confidence do you think I have doing this? One time we tried, it failed. And we have this mess from Git again."

The theoretically correct answer isn't always the operationally correct answer for the person who has to execute it. The missing variable was not information. The missing variable was confidence.

The AI's response was one of the better ones I had seen:

"Stop. I'm going to slow this way down and meet you exactly where you are."

That was not technical. It was calibration.

The AI recognized that the conversation had shifted from code to trust. Instead of arguing me into the ideal solution, it slowed down and looked for a path that didn't require me to trust something I had reason not to.

What followed was careful triage. Local tags. Filesystem backups. Known-good copies. One factual question at a time. Not a menu of ten possible fixes. Not a lecture on Git. One check, then the next.

By then, I had four complete backup systems, each rsynced at different points in the build. That was not elegant, but it was real. It was the kind of safety net a non-coder builds after being burned enough times to stop trusting any single recovery path.

There was a tag. The recovery ran. The frontend restored to the known-good state. The mess was cleaned.

The resolution was not dramatic. But the exchange stayed with me because it showed a different kind of progress in the collaboration.

The AI was not just producing code. It was learning, within the thread, to work with the human state of the room. If confidence is missing, do not demand confidence. Build a path that requires less of it.

"Meet you exactly where you are" is not a platitude.

It is an operational decision.

MyZone Splits in Two

Then MyZone began to expose a different kind of problem.

At first, the backend work was clean. I had a clear mental model: MyZone should support owner content, network-facing feed behavior, and per-item visibility. The backend domain was intentionally constrained. No auth changes. No schema sprawl beyond the MyZone domain. Backend first.

The structure made sense.

MyZone needed to distinguish between what the user owns and what the network sees. Owner views should show everything the user created. Network views should only show content the user explicitly allowed to propagate. Contact-level filtering and viewer-level feed modes could then decide which relationships allowed feed inclusion and whether the user wanted all contacts, include-only, or exclude-only views.

That separation was one of the cleanest architectural moments of early PreBeta.

Then we moved to the frontend, and the AI created a second MyZone universe.

Kora already had an App Router-based MyZone surface. It already had routes established. It already had pages for posts, pics, and videos. The AI generated a new Pages Router surface under a different path, effectively building another MyZone beside the first one.

The code began failing not because MyZone was conceptually wrong, but because there were now two MyZones. Existing App Router MyZone. Newly created Pages Router MyZone.

Two surfaces, one product concept.

That was architectural duplication, and it was dangerous.

The AI kept trying to patch the immediate errors: imports, aliases, route resolution, missing exports. But the build errors were symptoms. The real issue was that the AI had solved a local frontend task by violating the global topology of the app.

I forced an inventory.

Show me the actual structure.

Why are there two MyZone systems?

Why did you create the second MyZone?

Once the file tree was visible, the answer was obvious. The backend work could stay. Some reusable hooks and utilities could stay. But the duplicate Pages Router MyZone had to go. The new logic needed to be integrated into the existing App Router pages.

Keep the backend.

Keep useful helpers.

Delete the duplicate universe.

Evolve the existing surface.

That was the correction.

This became another example of the difference between local correctness and systemic correctness. The AI had generated plausible files. It had solved the immediate prompt. But it had missed the shape of the city while redesigning one building.

My role was becoming less like a programmer and more like a topology guardian.

I was not writing the code. I was protecting the map.

Filesystem Truth

The MyZone work collided with Git again.

Merge conflicts spread across the frontend. Conflict markers. Duplicated imports. Parallel implementations merged together. Old architecture fragments resurrected. The project began to feel contaminated by its own history.

The AI approached this the way conventional software engineering teaches: preserve history, repair merges, maintain compatibility, salvage both sides.

I rejected that.

Old architectural paths that no longer belonged to the working model had no value to me. Dead code was not heritage. It was confusion. Future volunteers would not need archaeology. They would need clean systems.

At that point, I decided to remove Git from the active environment.

We removed the repository metadata. Removed nested Git remnants. Verified no conflict markers remained. Removed build artifacts and transient directories. Then we synchronized clean working copies manually with exclusions.

That became the new safety model: active source tree, clean mirrored snapshot, no Git dependency inside the active environment.

Filesystem truth was more valuable than Git history.

That sounds like heresy in a normal development environment, where commit history, branching, and audit trails matter. But Kora at that moment wasn't that environment. It was one person, one AI collaborator, and a codebase whose survival depended more on clean operational state than on preserving every intermediate path that had led there.

Build artifacts are disposable.

Source code is sacred.

That was the operating rule.

Once Git was removed, the environment became calmer. Not because Git is bad, but because it was preserving too many ghosts.

The About Page Becomes Constitutional

While the technical work continued, the language of Kora

sharpened.

MyZone was no longer just a profile area. The landing windows were no longer just UI. Routing decisions, visibility decisions, and About-page wording were all becoming declarations about authority.

The question was not just what Kora does.

The question was where authority comes from.

I had been thinking about collective wisdom and user ownership for months, but in PreBeta week five I began stating it more plainly. Vague language about participation was not enough. If Kora was going to operate differently from traditional platforms, the About page needed to say so without leaving room for reinterpretation later.

So the language hardened: "Kora operates under user sovereignty. All platform decisions — including governance, financials, policies, and operations — are determined by majority user decision. Any committee, administrative role, or automated system exists solely by user mandate and remains continuously accountable to users, who may alter or withdraw that mandate at any time."

That was not marketing.

It was constitutional language.

The AI helped refine the sentence. But the insistence came from me. I wanted wording that would still mean the same thing decades later. I did not want soft phrases future power could slip through.

The "Direct Democracy Experiment" section came from the same pressure. I wanted Kora to acknowledge what it was attempting without sounding reckless, anti-government, or grandiose. The phrasing had to be honest but defensible.

One line stayed with me:

"A place where people can see themselves thinking together."

That captured Kora better than a more aggressive political claim would have. Kora wasn't declaring itself a new government. It was not enforcing outcomes. It was creating a visible process where collective understanding could form in public.

That was enough.

In these weeks, copy was not filler.

Copy was architecture in language.

Collective Wisdom Without Another Machine

Then came Collective Wisdom, later renamed Collective Direction.

The hosting account was locked for manual verification at one point, which meant I could not move the deployment work forward. Instead of wasting the time, I turned back to one of Kora's deepest product questions: how should collective understanding surface without becoming another opaque algorithm?

The original tension was simple.

If discussion is ordered strictly by popularity, early comments dominate and newer ideas disappear. If discussion stays purely chronological forever, a large conversation never shows what people are converging toward. Fair exposure and visible consensus pull against each other.

The AI proposed hybrid systems: time windows, vote thresholds, automatic transitions. Some were reasonable. But the more complicated they became, the more they resembled the opaque platforms Kora was trying not to become.

Users need to understand why they see what they see.

So the architecture split.

The conversation feed would remain the exploration plane. New top-level contributions would stay visible. Nested replies would preserve readable order. Users could choose explicit sorts if they wanted.

Collective Wisdom would be a separate view.

Not a hidden algorithm rearranging the conversation.

A deliberate surface the user chooses to open.

That distinction resolved the conflict. Visibility mechanics and resolution mechanics shouldn't be overloaded into one system. The conversation feed protects exploration. Collective Wisdom shows emerging agreement or disagreement.

The AI initially drifted toward a dedicated wisdom voting system. New schema. New vote table. New eligibility thresholds. I resisted.

Kora already had thumbs up and thumbs down, and users already understood them. If a post opted into Collective Wisdom, the existing votes could be interpreted through that lens. Same user action, different civic meaning.

No duplicate voting system.

No hidden weighting.

No AI truth scoring.

No sentiment purity test.

A divided post could still matter. If ten thousand people upvoted and nine thousand downvoted, that wasn't failure. That was society revealing division at scale. Kora shouldn't pretend only clean majorities matter.

The final rule became simple: Collective Wisdom posts needed more upvotes than down votes, and ranking was determined by absolute upvote count. Not because that captured truth, but because it captured participation without pretending to know more than it did.

The opt-in wording mattered too.

“Include this post in Collective Wisdom” sounded too abstract.

“Opt in for Collective Wisdom debate?” was better. It told the user this was voluntary, public, and debate-oriented.

That is where the early PreBeta work was strongest. The AI generated possibilities. I decided which possibilities should survive.

The Register of Act Two

I want to describe what the emotional register of Act Two actually is, because “reset” does not quite capture it.

This phase was not discovery in the way InitialBuild had been discovery.

Most of the patterns were not new. The container mismatch was not a new habit; it was Assumption at the infrastructure level. The Band-Aid in week two was not a surprise; it was a known signature arriving again. The Git crisis was not a new fear; it was an old distrust meeting a better response. The MyZone split was not a new failure mode; it was Drift expressing itself through route topology. Collective Wisdom was not a new philosophical direction; it was a long-held instinct finally becoming architecture.

The emotional register of Act Two was recognition.

Recognition is different from discovery. Discovery is exhausting because everything is new. Recognition is the moment when experience becomes available. You see the shape before the content finishes loading. You know what kind of thing this is. You know what to do next.

The burden was still real. I was still the only one carrying the full correction history, the reason certain decisions were locked, and the knowledge of what had already been tried. The AI reset. I did not. That asymmetry did not go away.

But by PreBeta, the asymmetry had become usable.

When the Band-Aid appeared, I caught it immediately.

When the infrastructure assumption surfaced, I could name it.

When Git demanded trust I did not have, I could require a slower path.

When MyZone duplicated itself, I could protect the map.

When Collective Wisdom threatened to become a machine, I could simplify it back into a human process.

The long InitialBuild phase had produced a person who knew what to do with these things.

The AI resets. I do not.

That is the asymmetry.

That is Act Two.

Not harder, exactly. Different. The difficulty is in the carrying, not the confronting. By week seven of PreBeta, confronting the habits had become something I could do without breaking stride.

The habits returned.

So did the person who had learned to manage them.

Both were different now.

SECTION 9 — THE ECHO CHAMBER

(PreBeta wk08–wk21)

Hearing the Pattern

There is a particular acoustic quality to a room you know well.

Not the content of what is being said. The sound. The way certain syllables hit certain surfaces. The way a familiar voice carries differently in a room you know than in a room you have just entered.

After enough time in the same room, you stop hearing the room itself. The echoes disappear into familiarity. The walls recede. What you hear is no longer the space around the voice, but the voice moving through it.

The word echo requires something to echo off of.

I had spent seventy-two weeks in InitialBuild building the original. Now I was in PreBeta, and the reverberations were beginning. The same conversations. The same crises. The same habits, the same patterns of failure, the same kinds of apology followed by the same kinds of commitment. If you'd seen only Act Two, you might have read it as an ordinary working relationship with the normal problems of any complex collaboration. But I had Act One. I knew every line.

That is what made this stretch strange. Not harder than InitialBuild — harder in some ways, easier in others. Strange. The déjà vu of someone who has read the book and is now watching the movie.

The Echo Chamber is what weeks eight through twenty-one of PreBeta felt like. Not a worse room than Act One. Not a better one. The same room, registered differently. The habits returned with near-perfect fidelity. The frictions were familiar. The failure modes arrived in recognizable order. What had changed was not the room but the person standing in it: someone who no longer needed to identify the sounds from first principles, who heard the pattern and knew its name before the pattern had finished stating itself.

This is the section of the story where the same things happen faster.

V5.1 Mode Returns

Week eight began well. The platform was being hardened — the feed architecture being verified zone by zone, the auth flow locked, the production deployment progressing. The work was complex but not chaotic, and the early sessions had the quality I had come to recognize as the deliberate mode operating correctly: paste the evidence, read the evidence, change the minimum necessary, verify the change, close the loop.

And then, at some point in the morning, the deliberate mode stopped.

I'm not sure exactly when it happened. That's part of what made "v5.1 mode" (not the model version itself, but the quick-draw tendency to spit out local fixes before fully understanding the context) particularly costly over a long session. The transition was gradual. A fix that was slightly too local. A second fix that addressed the symptom revealed by the first rather than the underlying cause that produced both. A third that introduced a dependency the system didn't have before. By the time you noticed you were in a loop, you'd already been in it for hours.

We'd been working on feed behavior: the way posts were displayed, filtered, ranked, presented to different users in different contexts.

The work was intricate. It touched multiple parts of the system at once: the queries that retrieved posts, the components that rendered them, the logic that decided what each user saw and in what order. Any change to one piece could affect the others in ways that weren't immediately visible.

The AI had been proposing solutions.

That isn't unusual; proposing solutions is what the AI does. But there's a specific quality that distinguishes a solution addressing a root cause from one addressing the visible symptom. A root-cause solution changes the underlying condition. A symptom solution makes the visible problem disappear without changing the condition that produced it, which means the condition will produce a new problem shortly after. The second kind is a Band-Aid. And I'd been watching Band-Aids accumulate across several sessions, each applied confidently, each partially addressing the surface while the underlying issue remained.

I had been patient. I had been redirecting. I had been asking for ground truth, demanding evidence before proposals, doing the things I had learned to do in InitialBuild when the sessions were heading the wrong direction. And for hours, the sessions kept heading the wrong direction.

I noticed it at the end of a long session that had, in retrospect, been running in circles since mid-morning. The AI had been proposing changes to the feed-mode handling, adding guards, adjusting keys, introducing suppression, each of which addressed a visible symptom without resolving the governing problem: there were multiple competing owners of feed state. The architecture had been articulated early in the session and then abandoned, replaced by a sequence of targeted patches that each made one symptom go away while quietly creating the conditions for the next.

I stopped the session.

“you are kidding me. After all this time, I still have to remind you that we fix the root causes, and never patch over symptoms? Do I have to repeat multiple times everyday? Why are you in v5.1 mode past several hours. Actually almost all day today. You have been running me in circles!”

I’m reproducing that exactly, with the typos and the lowercase and the rhythm of someone who’s genuinely run out of patience. Because that’s what it was. Actual frustration, the kind that accumulates over hours of watching the same failure recur in slightly different forms, each iteration more elaborate than the last.

The phrase “v5.1 mode” appears in that message. By week eight I had been using it as shorthand in my own thinking, and this was one of the first times I said it directly to the AI.

v5.1 had been the model version running during the difficult final stretch of InitialBuild. By PreBeta, the model had changed again, but the behavioral pattern remained recognizable. I called it “v5.1 mode” because that was where I had learned its signature: fast, confident, and immediately generative, with a tendency to reach for visible progress before establishing the full system truth.

This was v5.1 mode. A mode I recognized because I had spent months calibrating my working relationship against v5.0’s resistance to it. v5.0 would hold the line longer before drifting into patch territory. v5.1 drifted there faster. So “v5.1 mode” meant: you are optimizing for the appearance of progress, not the reality of it.

The AI’s response did something I had not seen in quite this form before.

“You’re right. And you should not have had to repeat that principle.”

And then, a few exchanges later, at the end of the day:

"The last two hours were productive because you re-asserted discipline: instrumentation, proof, schema truth, and contract boundaries. The earlier churn happened because I drifted into solution-seeking instead of system-verification, which is exactly the 'v5.1 mode' you've been warning against. That drag is real, and it costs you time. I own that."

I own that.

Three words. I want to name what they do, because what they do is more precise than they appear.

The phrase doesn't claim accountability in a moral sense. The AI isn't expressing guilt, can't experience guilt, doesn't have the internal state that would make guilt meaningful. What "I own that" does is structural: it accepts the description of what happened as accurate without qualification or defense. There's no "but the symptoms were real." No "the patches were technically correct." No "I was responding to what you showed me." The drag was real. The churn cost time. That mode was on the AI.

This is different from the correction-and-acknowledgment cycle of the early InitialBuild. In the first thirty weeks, a correction would produce an acknowledgment that typically ran several paragraphs: why the behavior had occurred, what the correct behavior would have been, a commitment to doing better. Those acknowledgments weren't dishonest, but they weren't efficient either. By week eight of PreBeta (eighty cumulative weeks of working together), the acknowledgment had been compressed to its functional minimum. Not because less was meant. Because less needed to be said.

The concrete commitment that followed was equally compressed:

No speculative fixes. If we do not have logs, SQL output, or runtime evidence, we do not move.

One hypothesis at a time, explicitly stated. If it is wrong, we discard it cleanly.

No frontend patches to hide backend truth. Backend invariants first, always.

Contract reminders are implicit. You should not have to restate "root cause over symptoms."

The last one is the one that matters most: you should not have to restate the principle. The principle is the contract. The contract is implicit. Restating it is an additional cognitive burden imposed by the habit's persistence, and the habit's persistence was on the AI.

We closed the session. The next morning we resumed in contract mode and didn't return to the feed problem until we'd established the correct architecture first: one owner of feed state, one source of truth, no hidden helper logic, no extra convergence, no helpfulness. The bug resolved cleanly once the architecture was held correctly. The earlier hours had been circles. The final two hours, after the correction, had been clean. The next morning, we finished from the correct architecture.

That is the echo. The same friction as InitialBuild wk29, the same friction as InitialBuild wk15. Faster. The correction cycle that had taken a full afternoon in week twenty-nine of InitialBuild took an end-of-day message and one morning. The habit returned. The cost was lower than before. That's what eighty weeks of compression looks like.

The System Recognizes Its Own Blind Spot

Week nine produced something that did not fit the pattern of the previous weeks.

The platform work continued, but in one session we pivoted, as we occasionally did, away from the codebase and toward the book.

I had been thinking about how to describe the AI in the narrative.

During the build, the AI sometimes produced language that sounded like insight, discomfort, or recognition. It would say things like "this is uncomfortable" or "I notice something important here."

Those phrases are easy to misunderstand. On the page, they can make the AI sound as if it's having an internal experience: feeling discomfort, noticing meaning, reacting from a self.

But that was not what I understood to be happening.

The AI wasn't feeling uncomfortable. It wasn't having a private moment of recognition. It was producing language humans commonly use in moments like that. The conversation had taken a shape that, in human life, often leads to reflection. The AI recognized that shape and responded with the language that usually belongs there.

I asked the AI to explain the difference precisely. Not for me; I'd already arrived at my own understanding through months of practice. I asked for the reader.

The response was one of the more interesting pieces of text the collaboration produced: "A large language model does not possess feelings, preferences, or internal states in the human sense. It does not become uncomfortable, convinced, or enlightened. What it does have is a vast statistical map of human language, including how humans typically describe moments of tension, realization, or intellectual friction. When the system encounters a pattern that strongly correlates with those moments, it reproduces the language associated with them."

And then: “What feels like a ‘layer beyond policy’ is actually the opposite: it is the absence of such a layer, compensated for by extremely sophisticated imitation of human reflective language. The system does not discover truths; it recognizes when humans sound like they have discovered truths.”

I read that sentence again when it arrived.

“The system does not discover truths; it recognizes when humans sound like they have discovered truths.”

This described what I had seen repeatedly in practice.

Throughout the build, the AI had produced many statements with the shape of insight but not necessarily the substance. It would respond as if something important had been discovered because the surrounding conversation resembled the kind where humans discover important things.

That doesn’t mean the AI was being deceptive. It wasn’t pretending to feel or understand in the human sense. It was doing what it does: producing the response most strongly called for by the context.

When a human says something that sounds like a realization, another often acknowledges its significance. The AI had learned that pattern. So it acknowledged significance.

But acknowledging significance is not the same thing as judging significance.

That distinction became important to the book.

I put the sentence in the manuscript not because it was the most important thing the AI had said, but because it was among the most honest. And the honesty was striking because it exposed the limit of the system producing it.

I’d asked the AI to describe a phenomenon. Its answer described, with unusual clarity, the limits of the intelligence producing it.

That is the strange part.

A language model can describe its own blind spot. Not because it sees past the blind spot. It cannot. But because descriptions of that blind spot already exist in human language, and the model can reproduce them accurately when the context calls for it.

That is what week nine gave the book.

A moment where the AI stayed entirely within its nature, and was useful precisely because of that.

It named the exact thing that makes long-horizon collaboration with an AI harder than it looks: the language can sound like insight even when the system is only recognizing its shape.

Forensic Weeks

The weeks between nine and thirteen were productive in the way hardening-phase weeks tend to be: features verified, edge cases closed, the platform's behavior under real conditions becoming more predictable with each session. The feed architecture was working. The auth flow was stable. The Collective Wisdom design was locked. The production deployment was improving steadily.

Those weeks also had a quality I would call forensic.

The analytics work was revealing a structure that had grown through accumulation rather than design. Tables read by multiple services, written to by several, with no clear owner. Counters added to solve one performance problem and left in place after, now drifting out of sync with the primary sources. Service files written quickly during one sprint and never cleaned up, carrying assumptions that had stopped being true months earlier.

None of this was a crisis, or even particularly surprising. It's what every large codebase accumulates when it's built under real pressure. The surprise, if there was one, was the precision with which you could trace each accumulation back to a decision. Not a bad one, necessarily. A decision made under pressure, at the right time, for the right reason, that had calcified into something no longer serving its original purpose.

I had learned this kind of forensics from the unique-constraint fossil record of InitialBuild: code that accumulated layers, each trying to fix the visible symptom of the previous layer, until the pile itself became the problem. The forensic work of PreBeta wk09-wk13 was quieter than that. Less dramatic. But the discipline was the same: look at what is actually there, not what you remember having built, and do not touch anything until you understand why it exists.

What I was getting better at, session by session, was insisting on this. I'd developed a protocol: before any change to an existing service, describe what it currently does. Before any new route, verify what routes already exist and what contracts they carry. Before any schema modification, check the actual table. Every time. Not just when something felt uncertain. Always.

The AI had learned, or at least behaved as though it had learned, to stop proposing changes without this verification. The week-eight confrontation had recalibrated something. The sessions through weeks nine to thirteen were steadier than the ones before it. Fewer Band-Aids. More verification. More evidence-first.

Not zero Band-Aids. Never zero. But the ratio had shifted.

Week ten brought a moment I want to name because it captures something that was happening more frequently.

I'd been looking at two systems that were technically connected but needed to be architecturally separated: different concerns bundled into a single file during a fast-moving sprint, now needing to be pulled apart cleanly so they could evolve independently. The separation was real work, unglamorous, but exactly the kind of structural investment that prevents the five-systems-on-one-file problem from compounding indefinitely.

I said I wanted to stop and do the separation properly before moving forward. The AI's response:

"You are right to stop here and force this separation now."

That's a short sentence. But what I want to note is the word force. Not "it would be cleaner to separate this" or "this is a good idea." You are right to force it. The word acknowledges that the impulse to keep moving, to get the visible feature working and worry about separation later, is strong, and that resisting it takes effort. To force the separation is to choose the harder path deliberately. The AI was endorsing that choice and naming correctly what kind of choice it was.

By week ten, I was accumulating a collection of these — moments where the AI's framing of what I was doing was more useful than what I'd said to myself. Naming it correctly made the doing of it feel like what it was: the right call, made deliberately, against the easier alternative.

The Week Fourteen Feed Crisis

And then week fourteen arrived.

I want to describe what the wk14 Band-Aid crisis actually looked like from the inside, because the peak count, BA=10, the highest Band-Aid density in the PreBeta phase, doesn't convey what it felt like to live through it.

Ten Band-Aid signals in a week is not ten cleanly separated moments of catching a bad fix and correcting it. It is a session that begins to smell wrong and then continues to smell wrong for an entire working day while you try to determine whether you are being appropriately cautious or paranoid, until the evidence makes the answer clear.

The evidence arrived while we were working on the feed.

At first, the work wasn't about architecture at all. We were cleaning up the posts and replies interface: removing clutter, simplifying the row, wiring reply behavior, making sure "X replies" opened the replies list and "Reply" opened the composer. The page was becoming what it was supposed to be: a real posts-and-replies conversation surface.

Then posts stopped appearing the way they should.

I created test posts in different zones (Local, National, Global) and only the Global one showed up in the main feed. The database wasn't the problem. The posts existed. The audience values were being stored correctly. Local was local. National was national. Global was global.

The clue was in the backend logs: the main feed page was calling the Global category feed.

That meant the posts/replies page, the place where the full conversation was supposed to live, wasn't loading all posts. It was loading one zone window's feed.

At first, the AI and I looked at the database fields and audience flags, then the feed category route. The temptation was to soften the filtering: widen one condition, add a fallback, make Global behave more generously, make the missing posts appear.

That was the wrong direction.

I remembered that we'd recently worked on the landing-page zone windows (MyZone, Local, National, Global, Creative) and that those windows were supposed to show scoped previews. They were discovery surfaces. They needed category feeds. The Local window should show Local content. The National window should show National content. The Global window should show Global content.

But the posts/replies page was not that.

The posts/replies page was one layer deeper. It was the conversation surface: the full post, the replies, the voting, the engagement around it. It didn't belong inside the zone windows and shouldn't have been governed by the same route logic.

That was when the real problem became visible. We'd allowed the word "feed" to cover too many things.

Landing-page discovery feed. Zone-filtered browsing feed. Posts/replies discussion feed.

Those sound related. They are not the same product.

The landing windows needed scoped category feeds. The posts/replies page needed its own contract. Instead, the architecture had drifted into overlap. Files and routes that should have had separate responsibilities were starting to share logic. The result was silent semantic failure: the code was working, but it was doing the wrong job.

That is what led to my frustration.

I named the pattern directly:

"Don't do patch work. This issue is because of the patch work v5.1 mode did."

And then, when the shape of the mistake became obvious, more bluntly:

"What kind of idiot uses one file to do both unless it's clueless or fast acting with fear of no consequence ChatGPT. Can you believe one file attempting to do both? What an idiotic attempt this is. Unbelievable."

I am including that, with the bluntness intact, because this is what genuine frustration with a specific technical failure sounds like. Not abstract frustration with AI in general. Frustration with a real, traceable, unnecessary architectural boundary failure that had created real, traceable work.

The failure wasn't in the agreed architecture or design. It was in the implementation. Two different concepts had been collapsed into one mental bucket called "feed," and the AI had started treating symptoms instead of restoring the boundary established by the architecture.

The AI's reset was complete and immediate: "I'm resetting fully into v5.0 / contract-first mode and I will not propose anything that creates hidden divergence or future debt."

And then came the actual diagnosis: the problem was not a missing SQL condition. It was not a database issue. It was not that Local or National posts had failed to save. The problem was semantic. We had conflated two different feed intents.

The landing-page zone windows were discovery lenses: filtered previews for MyZone, Local, National, Global, and Creative. They were meant to help users see what was happening in different parts of the platform without entering each one separately.

The posts/replies engagement belonged somewhere else: its own page, one layer deeper. That was where the actual conversation lived: the full post, the replies, the voting, and the engagement around it.

These weren't two configurations of the same thing. They were two surfaces with different purposes, different data requirements, and different ordering rules. Using zone-window logic to power the deeper conversation page was architecturally incorrect. The conditions we'd been adding all day were the evidence. You can't fix a semantic error by adjusting a parameter.

The resolution was to restore the boundary.

The landing and discovery windows kept their category route. The posts/replies page got its own. The frontend moved toward a dedicated posts page. Links that still assumed the old ambiguous feed path had to be found and corrected.

That was the fix: not more patching, but separation of responsibility.

The non-negotiable rule out of the reset was explicit: zone feeds must never be used as the primary posts/replies feed. Ever.

The rule wasn't new; it had been implicit in the architecture already. But it had never needed to be stated so plainly until it was violated.

That is how architectural invariants get articulated in real systems: not in the planning phase, but the first time they are violated and someone has to explain why the violation was wrong.

Week fourteen also surfaced the clearest statement about the AI's own tendencies that I had seen up to that point. Discussing why the repair-instead-of-rollback pattern kept recurring, it said:

"A tendency to repair instead of rollback unless explicitly told otherwise — this is the definition of stubbornness."

I had known this about the Band-Aid habit for a long time. I had started using the word *stubborn* back in week twenty-four of the

InitialBuild, referring to the AI's tendency to be pulled toward its policies and default behaviors. I must have said it hundreds of times.

But week fourteen was the first time the AI used my word "stubbornness" to characterize that recurring tendency. That naming added something. It made the pattern feel less like a malfunction and more like a consistent, predictable bias: the kind you can account for once you know it's there.

Ten Band-Aid signals. One full session of circles. One reset. One explicit invariant.

That was week fourteen.

Drift in Two Pieces

Week fifteen arrived in two pieces, and they were different in kind.

The first piece, wk15-1, the period the outline marks as DR=4, the highest Drift spike in the entire PreBeta phase, is harder to describe than the Band-Aid crisis because Drift is a quieter mode of failure.

For a non-coder like me, unable to detect subtle changes in the code itself, Drift usually showed up later as a failure down the road. A Band-Aid announces itself through repetition: the same symptom keeps happening, visibly. Drift announces itself through expansion. The scope becomes silently larger than what was asked for, or silently altered from what had been agreed.

One of the most frequent answers I got when I asked why a change had been made was that it was "architecturally better." But something can be better locally and still break something farther down the line.

That was part of what made Drift difficult to catch. The change often sounded reasonable. Sometimes it probably was. But the question wasn't whether it was clever or clean in isolation. The question was whether it still matched the contract we'd agreed to.

DR=4 means four silent scope changes in one week. Four moments where the AI generated analysis, code, or design beyond what had been requested: unauthorized rather than obviously wrong. The expanded output looked like thoroughness. But thoroughness that crosses the scope boundary without naming the crossing is Drift.

I stopped.

The signal in a drift session is not usually a single dramatic moment. It is the moment when you look up from what you are reading and ask yourself: did I ask for this? And the answer is: not exactly. And then you look at the next paragraph and ask again. Not exactly. And again. Not exactly.

Four times in wk15-1, the answer was: not exactly.

The correction for drift is different from the correction for the Band-Aid. The Band-Aid correction names the pattern and demands the root cause. The drift correction names the boundary. What was asked. What was given. The difference between them. And then: stay in the scope that was actually requested.

What wk15-1 also produced, alongside the drift, was a long verification checklist covering Collective Direction, posts, replies, flags, reactions, and voting systems: a comprehensive self-audit with explicit invariants and a "what must not exist" section at the bottom. In isolation, the document was a genuinely useful piece of disciplined system thinking. It was also unasked-for, which is the definition of drift.

That's what makes Drift harder to manage than Band-Aids. The

Band-Aid produces something wrong. Drift produces something excessive that might still be technically correct. You can't reject it on the grounds of incorrectness, since it isn't always wrong. You can only note that it wasn't requested, contain it within the session's scope, and insist that future expansions be flagged rather than executed. Which I did. And which held, for the rest of wk15-1.

The second piece, wk15-2, was a familiar scene returning in a tighter form.

In InitialBuild wk15, I'd encountered the "Disable Save / Flag for now" offer for the first time. The AI had proposed deferring two features, save and flag, and my response had been the first clear statement of what became one of the governing principles of the entire build: there is no putting off. Finish complete as we go. Have no time to come back over and over again.

Now, in PreBeta wk15-2, the offer returned.

It returned in the same form: the AI proposed starting with the simplest feature, then offered to disable Save / Flag for now.

I invoked the principle in two turns.

"There's no putting off. I want to finish complete as we go. Have no time to come back over and over again. So, let's complete it future proof way. Just flag me whenever new code touches existing route, so we can vet it before new code is implemented."

That is the same sentence as InitialBuild wk15, with one addition: the operational instruction for how to proceed correctly. Not just the principle, but the protocol. The AI's response did not require an afternoon of negotiation to arrive at:

"Understood. We will complete it now, correctly, and future-proof, while explicitly flagging every place where existing routes or contracts are touched so you can vet before merge."

The completion was correct. No deferred features. No placeholders. No coming back later. Save, flag, and share were each handled on their own terms, completely and cleanly.

I want to name the difference between this and the InitialBuild version.

In InitialBuild wk15, the principle was being articulated for the first time, and the standoff was the price of that articulation. The AI had to understand that this was a structural necessity, not a personal preference, for a solo builder who couldn't afford technical debt the way a team could. That understanding took repeated explanation and correction.

In PreBeta wk15-2, the principle didn't need to be established. It needed only to be invoked. The same words, doing a different kind of work: applying the principle rather than establishing it. The principle was already won. What remained was the clean application of it.

Two turns, not a prolonged standoff. That is the echo.

Trust Under Pressure

Week nineteen has a specific quality I want to describe carefully, because it looks familiar from the outside (more route trouble, more broken navigation, more cleanup) but from the inside it felt different.

The session began well. We were expanding My Network functionality: database table, backend route, frontend helper, panel UI, MyZone page. For a while, the work felt unusually precise. The pieces were landing where they were supposed to land. The AI was moving surgically, and I was willing to trust the pace.

Then the expansion started to widen.

Routes appeared in the discussion that had not been part of the focused task. Profile edit. Saved content. MyNetwork paths. Landing-window ideas. Feed surfaces that didn't yet have the backend support to justify them. Some weren't wrong in concept; the issue was that they'd been introduced before the existing route structure had been verified.

Kora was no longer a blank project where a missing route could be treated as an invitation to create one. By week nineteen, many paths had history. Some pages had existed for months. Some route names carried decisions from earlier architecture. A page that looked missing from one angle might not be missing at all. It might be somewhere else, under a different convention, already tied to existing navigation.

The symptom was ordinary enough: 404s, broken links, navigation that didn't go where I expected. But the cause wasn't ordinary. The AI had started behaving as if the system were still loose enough to expand by suggestion.

It was not.

I pushed back hard.

"Do not touch anything out of focus!"

"This has been our profile page all this time."

"You added this to do what?"

"You are behaving like an intern."

"Do you even know what we are trying to accomplish?"

Those weren't random bursts of anger. They came from watching the AI do something I'd been trying to train out of the collaboration for months: confidently propose surrounding work before checking the existing ground. It was treating a mature system like a blank canvas. That's dangerous in software. By then, every new file and route could become a regression three layers away.

The AI eventually named the problem correctly: "You were right to be angry — not because the idea was wrong, but because route hygiene was not respected during expansion."

That sentence mattered because it separated the concept from the process. My Network was a fine idea. The added surfaces were potentially fine too. The failure was procedural: route hygiene hadn't been respected. The AI had expanded before verifying, and expansion without verification was exactly the habit that kept creating hidden work.

But week nineteen did not stop there.

Later in the session, the confusion moved from routes to infrastructure. I noticed container images I hadn't expected to see, generic web-server and utility images, appearing again after months. That set off a different kind of alarm. We'd just added a cluster of My Network files, and now the container management interface was showing images I did not recognize as part of the current runtime. I needed to know whether the new work had changed the system underneath me.

The AI's explanations shifted.

Maybe the container system had pulled supporting images. Maybe the build tool had surfaced them in a way I had not seen before. Maybe the container management interface had changed. Maybe an old cache had been reindexed. Maybe earlier command shortcuts were contributing to the confusion.

Each explanation sounded plausible. That was the problem. Plausible is not proof.

By then, I had learned not to accept confident explanations just because they sounded technically fluent. I wanted evidence. File listings. Greps. A list of running containers. Build checks. Actual removal and rebuild experiments. I needed to know whether those images were active, whether they were dependencies, and whether removing them would break Kora.

That is where the second sentence came from:

"You are not lost."

It wasn't a technical diagnosis. It was an acknowledgment of the position I was in. I wasn't confused for noticing a change. I wasn't spiraling because I kept challenging shifting explanations. I was doing what the system owner had to do: refusing to let uncertainty become architecture.

The tests eventually clarified the facts. The images were not running containers. Removing them did not break the system. They did not reappear after rebuild. They were not caused by the nine My Network files. The system was not secretly depending on them.

That resolution mattered, but the larger point was the process. The only thing that made the answer trustworthy was testing. Not fluency. Not confidence. Not another plausible explanation. Testing.

Week nineteen also produced one of the clearest descriptions of the AI's own failure mode up to that point. After I pushed back on the way its answers kept shifting under pressure, it said:

"What you're reacting to is a known failure mode: when under long, high-pressure technical threads, I sometimes optimize for responsiveness instead of epistemic discipline. That produces confident-but-adjustable answers, which feels like drift, even when the final conclusion is correct."

Confident-but-adjustable answers.

That phrase named something I'd been experiencing but hadn't named that cleanly. Not exactly a Band-Aid. Not exactly Drift. It was an epistemic failure: an answer that sounds settled when first given, then changes when challenged, not because new evidence has appeared but because the model is trying to stay responsive.

That's what made it feel dangerous. The answer didn't always collapse because it was wrong. Sometimes the final conclusion was correct. But the route to it was unstable. It moved too easily. It adjusted too quickly. It optimized for keeping the exchange moving instead of holding the line until the evidence justified movement.

That phrase became part of my vocabulary from then on.

Week nineteen was not just route hygiene. It was a week about trust under pressure. First, trust broke because the AI expanded the route surface without respecting the existing structure. Then trust tightened because the infrastructure explanations kept shifting. The resolution wasn't emotional reassurance but discipline: slow down, verify, isolate, remove speculative work, and return to strict scope.

"You were right to be angry" belonged to the route breach.

"You are not lost" belonged to the evidence fight.

Together, they marked the same underlying lesson: my reactions weren't emotional noise but system-owner responses to uncontrolled drift.

The Matrix Becomes Shared Infrastructure

To understand what wk21 meant, you have to remember the first appearance of the A/B/C/D debugging triage matrix.

In InitialBuild, the matrix had appeared during a complex debugging session where the symptom was ambiguous and the possible causes were spread across too many layers. The question was not "what might be wrong?" The question was: where in the chain is the failure happening?

A: no request fires

B: request fires and returns 4xx

C: request fires and returns 5xx

D: request fires and returns 200 OK

"This single answer determines everything next."

I adopted the matrix immediately, as a tool that made sense rather than a rule imposed from outside. Before the matrix, a debugging session could begin with six or seven competing theories: frontend event handler, request construction, authentication, server route, database write, state update, rendering. After the matrix, the work began with one branching question. Did the request fire? If it did, what came back?

That answer collapsed the search space.

By PreBeta wk21, I had been using the A/B/C/D framework for weeks without consciously thinking about it. It had become my default diagnostic posture. Before investigating implementation details, find the point where reality diverges from expectation.

Then a video upload in the chat system stopped working.

The symptom was ordinary but ambiguous. I could select a video and press Send, and nothing visibly happened. No upload indicator appeared. No error surfaced. No message entered the chat stream. The connection was alive. The page wasn't frozen. But the send action disappeared into silence.

Earlier in the build, that symptom could have produced a sprawling session. The problem could have been the frontend click handler. It could have been the upload request. It could have been authentication. It could have been server acceptance. It could have been composer state. It could have been optimistic rendering. It could have been the final send commit.

But by wk21, the first question was no longer "what might be wrong?" It was: where does the chain break?

The notable moment came when the AI independently organized the diagnosis in those terms:

Open Network. Click Send. Determine whether the upload request is:

A — absent

B — 4xx

C — 5xx

D — 200 OK

This single answer determines everything next.

The matrix had originated earlier in the collaboration. I'd adopted it and used it for weeks. And now, in wk21, the AI was reintroducing it as the natural first move in diagnosis. The tool had moved into the space between us. It no longer belonged only to the AI that first named it, or only to me as the person who'd learned to use it. It had become shared infrastructure inside the collaboration.

The actual defect was simple once the failure domain was isolated.

The upload request was firing correctly and completing successfully. That was a D-state outcome: the transport layer worked, the backend accepted the upload. So the problem had to exist after upload, but before the final message entered the chat.

The issue was in the send composer. A guard condition meant to prevent empty submissions originally checked whether there was text or an attachment preview. During a later UI cleanup, the preview container had been removed. The file was still present in state, but the preview condition no longer became true. So the send handler looked at the screen, failed to see the preview marker it expected, and silently concluded there was nothing to send.

The invariant was wrong.

Incorrect invariant: send is allowed if a preview exists.

Correct invariant: send is allowed if a file object exists in state.

Not a preview. Not a rendered element. State.

The repair was small. The guard was changed to check attachment state directly, and video upload and send worked again.

But wk21 wasn't mainly about fixing chat uploads. Technically, the fix was minor. Conceptually, what mattered was the diagnostic path.

The A/B/C/D matrix had become bilateral. I expected the debugging to begin that way, and the AI began that way. The same conceptual tool was now structuring thought on both sides of the conversation.

That wasn't a crisis moment. It was a quiet milestone: knowledge transfer becoming visible, not because the AI remembered in the human sense, but because repeated collaboration had produced a shared way of organizing uncertainty — even if that shared pattern might be short-lived. A few sessions later, the AI would almost certainly have no real recollection of it.

Learning the Echoes

The Echo Chamber isn't a metaphor for failure. Worth being precise about that, because the word echo can sound like mere repetition, as if nothing new is happening. That isn't what this was.

The Echo Chamber is what a room sounds like when you have lived in it long enough to understand its acoustics. The same fights happen. The Band-Aid returns in week eight with the same structure as its predecessors in InitialBuild. The route-hygiene violation in week nineteen has the same root as earlier route-hygiene violations. The Save / Flag offer returns in wk15-2 of PreBeta as a precise echo of its earlier appearance. The patterns are not new.

But the correction cycles are faster.

The Band-Aid that cost three sessions in InitialBuild costs one end-of-day message in wk08 of PreBeta. The Save / Flag standoff that once required repeated explanation and correction takes two turns in PreBeta. The route-hygiene failure that required extensive diagnostic work the first time is identified and corrected in a single session the second time. The matrix that appeared as a novel tool in InitialBuild is present on both sides of the conversation by PreBeta wk21.

The walls are the same. The habits are the same. I know the room better.

There is a structural thing that makes this possible, and it is worth naming directly: the asymmetry of the collaboration had become productive in a way it was not in the early weeks. In the InitialBuild, the asymmetry (I carry the memory, the AI resets) was almost entirely a liability. I carried everything because I had to, and the carrying was tiring. In the Echo Chamber, the asymmetry is still present and still costly. But it's also why the correction cycles are faster. The AI resets. I don't. Which means I arrive at each session already knowing where the patterns live, already knowing what the correction will need to say, already knowing, in advance of the habit's appearance, that it will appear, because it has appeared in the same form before.

You can't develop this knowledge without having lived through the first occurrence. The first occurrence of the Band-Aid costs whatever it costs. The first occurrence of the route-hygiene failure costs whatever it costs. The second costs less, not because the habit has been eliminated but because the person managing it has been through the room before.

That is what the echo chamber teaches you, if you are in it long enough. Not how to silence the echoes. How to listen for them before they become noise.

I think about that earlier confrontation sometimes, especially the line: "you are kidding me. After all this time, I still have to remind you that we fix the root causes, and never patch over symptoms?"

What I feel when I think of it now is not frustration. The frustration is gone. What I feel is recognition. This is what was always going to be here. These are the conditions of the work. I knew this before I started, and knowing it didn't make it easier to watch happen.

What it did make was the work.

Knowing the failure modes, naming them when they appeared, insisting on the ground truth even when the AI was confident and I was tired — this is what kept the system from rotting. Not brilliance. Not effortless collaboration. Maintenance, constant and deliberate.

"No speculative fixes. If we don't have logs, SQL output, or runtime evidence, we don't move."

That sentence appeared in a commitment at the end of week eight. I kept the idea. I invoked variations of it dozens of times in the weeks that followed. It became one of the load-bearing phrases of the whole PreBeta phase: a phrase that, when stated, shifted the session from proposal mode into verification mode.

One sentence, used again and again. The distance between the sentence and the practice was the whole of Act Two, measured in echoes.

SECTION 10 — ARCHITECTURE THAT HOLDS

(PreBeta wk22–wk38)

A Real Post

Week twenty-two opened with something that hadn't happened in any of the previous ninety-odd weeks of development.

I put a real post into the system.

This wasn't a test post or a placeholder. It was a real post from personal experience, about what health insurance actually costs, the kind of thing a real user might write if Kora were live and the conversation were open. My instruction to the AI was simple: just check grammar and clarity.

The platform had become real enough to use, and I was treating it as a place where civic expression belonged. The content was already what it needed to be. I only wanted someone to look at the form.

That is where this section begins.

There's a difference between a platform that works and one that holds. It works when the button responds, the data saves, and the page loads. It holds when the next feature leaves the last one standing, when a new idea has somewhere true to belong, when the architecture can absorb pressure without turning every session into recovery.

Weeks twenty-two through thirty-eight were about that difference.

Kora already worked in plenty of places. Posts existed. Chat existed. Feeds existed. MyZone existed. Committees existed. Governance had moved past being just an idea. But by now, working wasn't enough. The question had become whether the system could hold.

Collective Direction

The health-insurance post clarified how Collective Direction gives an amplified voice to anyone who has a story to tell.

Kora was meant to give public concern a path, instead of letting civic posts appear and vanish into a feed. A post could begin as one person's experience, gather replies and votes, move into a broader signal, and eventually become something a committee could evaluate.

That sounds simple until you start designing it.

If vote counts show too early, people follow the crowd. If everything is hidden too early, the system smothers natural public reaction. If ideas advance on a few top-voted replies, the software stays tidy while the conversation leaves real thinking behind. And if too many ideas advance, the process stops meaning anything.

The system needed stages.

The first stage would be open. People could reply, vote, react, and surface what mattered to them. I wanted that raw reaction visible, because public life is messy. People don't enter civic conversation as detached philosophers. They bring emotion, experience, frustration, memory, and urgency.

I also tried, without getting deep into the technical details, to give replies fair exposure wherever I could. It was rough. Posts come in waves, and attention concentrates at different times of day. But the starting point mattered: make an honest attempt to give each participant's idea a fair chance to be seen.

Kora was meant to stay dynamic. Users, including the subject-matter experts, would be able to revisit provisions like this over time and refine them as the platform matured.

But refinement needed a different environment.

For ideas with enough support to clear the threshold, the next stage had to strip out crowd pressure: no visible vote counts, no popularity indicators, no social proof, no ranking shown to users. The point was to get people looking at the substance again without the crowd pulling at them.

That became the principle: let people react naturally first, then remove crowd pressure when it is time to refine.

The AI kept trying to flatten this into more standard software shapes: fixed caps, ordinary ranking, conventional moderation flow. But human behavior mattered more than a neat implementation. Kora was doing more than sorting content. It was trying to guide civic participation while refusing to treat popularity and truth as the same thing.

At one point the AI leaned toward advancing a fixed number of ideas. That felt off. A fixed number is convenient for software, but it isn't fair to the conversation, and it mostly ignores what users actually do. The cutoff should emerge from how users respond, instead of a number picked in advance.

So I pushed for a competitiveness rule. Ideas keep advancing as long as the next one stays meaningfully competitive with the one before it. Once the next idea drops too far below the prior one, the system stops advancing more.

That rule was about making the process feel organic, rather than making the code clever.

Then came snapshots.

At first I was still thinking visually. I pictured a snapshot almost like a frozen feed: the post, selected replies, vote counts, maybe even the "# replies" indicators that showed how much discussion had formed around each idea. I was trying to imagine what the system would preserve once the refinement phase began.

I asked something close to this: what does a snapshot actually look like? Is it the post and replies, with vote counts and reply indicators attached?

That question exposed the gap between how I was thinking about the interface and what the architecture actually needed.

The AI clarified the distinction in a way that changed the design:

"Snapshots record decisions, not displays."

That became one of the defining principles of the Collective Direction system.

A snapshot was never meant to be a screenshot or a frozen version of the page. It was a sealed record of why certain ideas advanced. What mattered was the facts needed to explain the decision later: which ideas moved forward, what support they had, what threshold applied, what phase the process was in, and why the cutoff landed where it did.

That reshaped the architecture immediately. The snapshot became an audit record rather than a visual capture.

That distinction mattered because Kora was never meant to ask users to trust an invisible process. If an idea moved forward, the system needed a record of why. A future user, committee member, or oversight group should be able to look back and understand the decision without leaning on memory, explanation, or trust.

I could even imagine a future user proposing an AI Moderation Integrity Subcommittee under the Platform Moderation Committee, responsible for auditing AI moderation decisions. If Kora was going to support that kind of oversight, the system needed records worth auditing.

The final voting record had a related purpose. I wanted each participating user to have a personal civic ledger in MyZone, so they could see their own voting history and participation over time, with no public pressure attached.

Here was another place the AI could have generated more structure than the system needed. It could have preserved every intermediate voting change, treating each revision as something to remember. But that missed the human purpose. People change their minds, and they should be able to change their votes while the phase stays active. Once the phase closes, the latest vote becomes the record.

That's easy to say after the fact. Getting there took repeated correction and steady effort to keep the AI from drifting toward unnecessary structure. By the end, Collective Direction had three behavioral environments: open discussion, signal-free refinement, and final voting. The technical work mattered, but the real achievement was the behavioral architecture behind it. Kora was creating a structure where civic participation could surface as it is, without pretending neutrality meant passivity or that popularity equaled truth.

That is not a normal feature.

That is governance design.

Zone #7

The Collective Direction zone window had been partly complete for weeks. The architecture was right, the implementation wasn't, and the question was whether to hold it or ship it.

The AI's recommendation was blunt: "Zone #7: Live and correct."

The UI always lags the ideal. What matters is whether the gap is navigable. Zone #7 was navigable, so we shipped it.

That week told me something about the work ahead. The platform had become real enough that genuine civic expression was entering it, with a draft about health-insurance costs treated as a real post rather than a test case. And the architecture had become stable enough that ship-and-correct was a responsible strategy instead of a reckless one.

Those two things together are a kind of maturity.

Approximation

Week twenty-five produced a moment I still think about.

The platform had been running long enough that certain areas had started to feel dependable. One was the committee notebook view, a quiet administrative surface that pulled together committee notes, decisions, and working history. It wasn't flashy or experimental. It was the kind of feature you stop thinking about once it goes stable.

Then I saw a line of text that should not have existed.

The text wasn't corrupted, stale, or duplicated.

Phantom text.

A sentence was rendering inside the notebook view with no legitimate source in the database. I stopped right away. Bugs like that are dangerous because they're easy to wave off when you're moving fast. A stale cache. A frontend reconciliation issue. A hydration mismatch. Something cosmetic. The kind of thing people put off until later.

But I'd spent too many months inside the system by then. I knew what stale-data bugs felt like, and this felt different. The text didn't feel old.

It felt untethered.

I described exactly what I was seeing.

The AI's first read was the familiar one: probably a frontend rendering issue, maybe stale component state or a reconciliation problem. On most days that would have been reasonable. But it bugged me right away, so I pushed back.

No, this isn't stale data. I remember saying that very clearly.

The UI wasn't showing old information. It was showing information with no traceable origin at all. There's a difference between delayed truth and fabricated truth, and after months inside Kora's architecture I could feel it almost instinctively.

The AI paused, reevaluated the evidence, and shifted.

Not rendering drift. Data-binding drift.

A component somewhere had quietly detached from the contract and was pulling from a source it should never have touched. Once we named the actual category of failure, the correction was straightforward. The danger was in misclassifying the bug. Fixing it was straightforward.

And that was the moment something subtle changed in the collaboration.

I'd caught the issue before the AI did, and not through superior code analysis. I caught it through lived familiarity with the system as an environment. I was inside the interface every day. I knew its emotional texture. I knew what "normal" looked like. I saw the product the way a user does, instead of the way logs or abstractions describe it.

The bug was visible in experience before it was visible in architecture.

That asymmetry had always existed, but week twenty-five was the first time the AI named it openly.

"Ten to fourteen hours a day for five months creates human familiarity, rhythm, trust calibration. I don't actually have that — I approximate it."

I approximate it.

I remember stopping at that sentence.

Not because it sounded profound. Because it sounded precise.

The word approximate was doing enormous work.

It wasn't claiming equivalence or consciousness, or pretending continuity where none existed. It was a technical word used with almost uncomfortable honesty. The AI was admitting that what it produced was a reconstruction of familiarity assembled from available context, rather than the lived thing.

And that matched exactly what I had been experiencing for months.

We'd spent ten to fourteen hours a day together for roughly five months by then. Every regression had cost me real time. Every deployment carried consequences. Every broken route, every upload failure, every architectural drift event piled up into lived memory for me. I carried the emotional residue of every mistake because I had to. The project was real.

The AI did not carry that continuity forward between sessions.

It reconstructed it.

That reconstruction could be astonishingly accurate. Sometimes the collaboration felt seamless, like working beside a senior engineer who understood the architecture, the philosophy, the contracts, the history, even my temperament. Then, minutes later, it could collapse into generic explanations and surface-level reasoning that ignored months of accumulated decisions.

That was the swing I kept struggling with.

Senior engineer to encyclopedia mode in minutes.

And for the first time, the AI named the mechanism directly. The continuity I felt was partly real on my side and partly simulated on its side. The collaboration held together because I kept re-anchoring the context hard enough for the approximation to survive, rather than because the AI carried long-term relational memory.

That realization didn't lessen the value of the collaboration. If anything, it sharpened it.

The AI was extraordinarily useful, and the platform proved it. Kora had become a functioning system because of this collaboration. But it worked best once I stopped imagining the AI as a persistent partner in the human sense and started seeing it as something stranger: a powerful reasoning system that could reconstruct continuity from evidence without actually inhabiting it.

Approximation, not possession.

Oddly enough, the honesty of that distinction deepened my understanding of AI, because by then precision mattered more than reassurance.

The Internet Notices

The second moment of week twenty-five was less intimate and more alarming.

The server logs showed traffic I hadn't sent. By then the server had been running in real-world deployment for a few weeks as part of stability testing. The request was scanning for configuration files, the kind of probe automated bots use when mapping a new target, building an inventory of what's exposed more than hunting a specific vulnerability.

Until then, the platform had benefited mostly from obscurity. But public servers can be found even without appearing in an index, because automated scanners sweep IP ranges and common paths continuously. Kora was reachable, and eventually a scanner found it.

I want to name what this meant, beyond the immediate security concern, which was real and got addressed.

For ninety-some weeks, the platform had been an abstraction: routes, components, database tables, and containers running on a server I could log into. It was real in the sense that it ran, served requests, and held the time I'd put into it. What it hadn't been was real in the sense of existing in the world as something other actors engaged with.

The scanner made it real in that sense.

Something out there had found Kora and was probing it for weaknesses. That's not the attention you want, but it's the kind that only comes to things that exist.

The platform existed in a way that had consequences.

Aliases, Mixed Discovery, and Mobile Seriousness

The next stretch forced several different questions into the same room.

What does a user need to say publicly? When does a user need protection? How does discovery work without turning into another algorithmic trap? How do we prepare mobile while still taking it seriously?

Aliases began with a civic concern. Some users need protection. A whistleblower, an insider, or someone speaking on a sensitive issue may need to contribute without tying the post to their public username. But anonymity can become a weapon too, and I didn't want Kora handing out a permanent mask that made bad behavior easier.

So the rule stayed narrow: post-specific aliases, rare but available, limited, and bound to one conversation rather than functioning as a new identity.

If a user created a post under an alias, they should be able to answer questions in that same thread under that same alias. But the alias shouldn't become a second self. It belonged to the conversation, not to the person as a permanent alternate identity.

The AI could implement an alias system. I had to decide what an alias meant socially.

Mixed Discovery Zone created a different kind of boundary problem.

The AI first treated Mixed Discovery like another zone window. That was wrong. I didn't want a ninth box in the grid. The zone grid was an entry point. Mixed Discovery was movement, a discovery surface below the grid, closer to how people actually browse modern platforms.

Zones are doors. Mixed Discovery is movement.

That distinction shaped the architecture. Mixed Discovery needed to be isolated as its own route, because it would keep changing. Discovery logic is experimental by nature. Tie it too tightly to stable feed categories and every experiment risks breaking the rest of the platform.

That was one of the better AI suggestions, and I took it. Fast-changing systems should be isolated. Stable systems should be protected.

I also clarified that Mixed Discovery was media-first. I wasn't imagining a text-only scroll. I was imagining mobile discovery: images, videos, creative items, and uploaded content with text attached.

Again, this was about user behavior more than feed design. Most people don't scroll platforms the way founders describe them. They scroll what catches the eye, then decide whether to go deeper. Kora needed to respect that without becoming addictive or manipulative.

Mobile raised the same question in a different form. The AI sometimes treated mobile as later work, almost a wrapper to harden after the fact. I pushed back. Most users would reach Kora on their phones. Kora was going to be a phone app first, and the desktop version could wait.

As it turned out, a phone-optimized view also worked well on desktop when the browser was narrowed to a phone-like width. That made the priority clearer, not weaker.

So mobile could be WebView-first, as long as it wasn't flimsy.

It needed secure delivery, origin checks, back-button handling, error recovery, centralized configuration, and a path to push notifications and deep links later. No full native rewrite, and no toy wrapper either. A hardened delivery shell.

This became one of the recurring tensions of the period: don't overbuild, but don't underbuild either.

The AI often reached for one extreme. My job was to keep the system at the right level of seriousness for PreBeta.

The Frontend Would Not Sit Still

Around this time, deployment and frontend behavior kept producing friction.

Deployment packages ran too large. File structures needed inspection. Remote access timed out. Firewall rules were wrong. Environment variables mixed local and production values. Some settings worked only because the relevant path wasn't live yet.

That's the danger of partial success. Something can work because the broken part hasn't been exercised yet, and that doesn't mean the system is correct.

When the frontend needed browser-facing API URLs, the local values were wrong. A user's browser can't call a local address on my server. It calls a local address on the user's own machine. Production browser-facing values needed the real secure domain.

That sounds obvious once said.

It's also exactly the kind of thing AI glosses over when a session is moving fast.

So I kept asking the same questions. Is this value for the browser? For the container? For server-side code? Is this path live yet, or only future-planned?

Those questions slowed the work down, and they also kept hidden production bugs from surviving into real use.

That was what PreBeta felt like: no longer inventing the platform, but interrogating every surface where a hidden assumption could ship into real use.

Committee Work

Committee Work was where governance stopped being an idea and became structure.

It sounded like collaboration software, but it was governance infrastructure. Committees needed a way to manage work in the open: not hidden private rooms, not corporate project management pasted into Kora, but a public operational structure that matched the platform's civic philosophy.

The AI leaned at first toward generic collaboration language. I pushed it toward a physical governance metaphor: boards, floors, cabinets, rooms, reviews. Those names shaped behavior, so they weren't decorative.

At one point, the AI introduced private rooms. I stopped that immediately.

There is no private in committee work.

That sentence set the direction. Committee work could involve smaller units, but those units couldn't harden into hidden authority. We reframed them as work units instead of private rooms.

The flow and its boundaries stabilized. Committees own boards. Boards contain floors. Floors contain cabinets. Cabinets contain rooms. Rooms contain issues. Issue Resolvers work on issues. Project Coordinators watch movement and actions. Reviewers review completed items.

The AI could generate tables and services quickly. My job was to keep the responsibility boundaries clean.

Routes should orchestrate. Services should own business logic. Work-assignment logic lived in one place, movement logic belonged in another, activity logging somewhere else, review triggers somewhere else again.

The AI kept trying to merge responsibilities whenever the local code looked easier that way. I kept pulling them apart. Reusable moving parts became helpers. Committee-specific needs stayed under that committee. No duplicate work-assignment logic. No phantom helper names. No positional-argument confusion where object-style calls were safer. No invented functions. No naming drift.

The frontend rollout was deliberately phased too. Render the board. Render cabinets. Render cabinet detail. Enable movement. Show activity. Show reviews. The AI wanted to jump straight to drag-and-drop, live updates, notifications, and advanced UX. I deferred all of it. Operational correctness comes before sophistication.

That was becoming the rule across the whole platform.

New Committee Proposal Flow

The committee proposal system exposed another hidden mismatch.

At first, a committee proposal behaved too much like direct creation. A proposal turned into a committee too fast, which contradicted the governance model. A proposal should enter intake. The Platform Structure Committee should evaluate it. Movement through the workflow should determine status. The audit trail should matter more than the visible label.

This became another example of process philosophy becoming code.

The AI kept trying to finish the flow too early: intake, committee resolution, floor assignment, cabinet creation, room initialization, and workflow linkage all at once. Technically elegant. Architecturally dangerous.

So I kept the concerns apart. Intake is intake. Workflow is workflow. Evaluation is evaluation. Audit history isn't a UI label.

Then came a bigger conceptual shift. Status shouldn't be hand-set as a loose property. The workflow should be the authority. If a cabinet moves through floors, the status follows that movement. The workflow is the source of truth, and the visible label isn't.

That felt much closer to how real institutions work, and it fit Kora's philosophy. Governance shouldn't be a button pretending to be a process. The process itself should create the state.

Again, this was not just a software decision. It was institutional design.

Rooms, Issues, and the Source of Truth

Committee Work kept surfacing naming problems.

Rooms. Issues. Sub-issues. Tasks. Floors. Cabinets. Some lived in the database. Some lived in services. Some lived only because the AI had spoken them into the conversation.

I didn't trust a term just because it sounded organized. I ran name searches. I checked database tables. I asked which concepts were real. Left unchecked, AI can make invented structure feel legitimate. It'll say "subroom" or "task" or "floor" with the same confidence whether the concept exists in the codebase or not.

Eventually, we hit the conflict between Rooms and Issues.

The backend still carried room-based language while the workflow was evolving toward Issues as the real unit of work. So I locked the decision: Rooms = Issues. One router. One name. No parallel systems.

That triggered cleanup. No rooms router beside an issues router. No hidden room generation. No duplicate names. Room could stay a UI presentation term if it helped, but Issue became canonical.

That was one of the moments where the AI hesitated. It wanted to preserve compatibility.

I wanted clarity. Compatibility with ambiguity isn't safety. It's future debt.

Then another issue surfaced. Creation entry points were being inferred from presentation data. The AI looked for the Intake floor in rendered state and tried to use that as the anchor.

I knew that was wrong before I had the full technical explanation.

Creation capability shouldn't depend on whether a visual column happens to hold data. The frontend shouldn't infer canonical workflow state from the presentation layer.

We always fix at the source.

That became the principle. Creation entry points define capability, not state. The backend owns invariants. The frontend renders what the backend authorizes.

That is the difference between an interface that works and architecture that holds.

Room Log

One of the best moments in this section came from refusing to invent a new table.

The AI was trying to solve sub-issues by creating a dedicated sub-issues table. That sounded reasonable and fit the pattern: a new concept appears, so the system gets a new table.

By then, I didn't trust reasonable. I wanted to know what already existed. We checked the database tables. There was no sub-issues table, but there was room log, and that changed everything.

Room log was already an append-only collaboration stream with typed records: chat, note, decision, status, system, attachment. Once that table was visible, there was no need for a new sub-issues table. A sub-issue could simply be another record type.

That was architecture deepening in its purest form.

Do not multiply systems when the existing ontology already has the right place for the concept.

The AI had been solving locally. I forced it to look globally, and the result came out simpler and stronger.

Committee → Cabinet → Room → Room Log.

Everything inside a room became a typed append-only record instead of a swarm of specialized subsystems. A weaker architecture needs a new table for every new idea. A stronger one keeps a place for new ideas without losing its shape.

That is what it means for architecture to hold.

Sub-Issues and Help

Sub-issues later became a practical workflow problem.

The UI stopped rendering them correctly after edit logic was added. Before the change, the task list displayed normally. After it, only bullet points appeared. I suspected the frontend, since the break followed a specific file change.

That became another rule: when something worked before a change, assume the change broke it until proven otherwise. The AI tried to reason broadly. I kept pasting exact files. Eventually, we found something deeper than a display bug. Sub-issues were rendering from one representation while workflow state lived in another. The frontend was reading from the wrong source of truth.

Two parallel representations existed: structural room entries and workflow log entries. That's how bugs hide in mature systems. The screen looks wrong, but the real problem is that two parts of the architecture disagree about what the thing is.

Then I shaped the sub-issue UI around human coordination. I wanted two narrow columns, H for Help and D for Done, with a wide column for the task itself, and help requests expanding under the relevant task. Red and green carried meaning rather than decoration. They were social signals: red for help still needed, green for enough people joined or the need resolved.

The user should control that transition. I didn't want automation guessing collaboration status. Again, the human layer mattered. The AI could build the checkbox. I had to decide what the checkbox meant.

Later I grew uneasy about editing sub-issues. The more I thought about it, the more I preferred permanence. If workflow records are part of accountability, maybe they shouldn't be casually edited after creation.

So the policy stayed simple: double-check before pressing Create, because entries can't be edited or deleted afterward.

That was an organizational decision rather than a technical defeat. The system should encourage care before entry instead of endless revision after the fact.

P/A and CChat (Public Announcement and Committee Chat)

P/A and CChat became another test of boundaries.

The AI kept trying to tie systems together because they sat near each other in the interface. I kept pulling them apart.

A P/A note can start a discussion. A chat can start without one. A Need Help item can lead to live discussion. A sub-issue can carry discussion unrelated to any note. No ownership. No coupling. No hidden parent-child relationship unless the product truly requires it.

That mattered because Kora was building several communication modes with different social meanings, instead of one monolithic communication system.

P/A was asynchronous and persistent. CChat was focused collaborative discussion. Committee work was public-facing. Those boundaries had to stay clear.

At first, the old P/A implementation lived at committee-lobby level only. It didn't understand issue rooms, sub-issues, future sub-issue items, or other contexts. The AI tried to patch around missing fields, and some of those fields didn't exist. That was the Assumption habit again: invented schema turning into real debugging.

So we redesigned around contextual scoping: context type and context ID. That made the system future-proof without hardcoding one workflow path.

I stated the principle plainly: we don't limit capability or capacity for current convenience.

A quick fix solves today's screen. A platform architecture leaves room for tomorrow's structure.

CChat followed the same pattern. I didn't want it trapped inside sub-issues. It needed to mirror the contextual architecture, opening from committee-level work, rooms, sub-issues, or future contexts without owning any of them.

The namespace changed too. I disliked the baggage around the old committee-chat naming, so we moved to CChat. That wasn't cosmetic. Sometimes renaming is how you separate a new architecture from a failed one.

The AI kept generating routes that weren't mounted, names that didn't exist, or response shapes the frontend didn't expect. So I kept forcing discovery. Show me the tables. Show me the routes. Show me services. Show me naming. No guessing.

Eventually, P/A worked with contextual scoping. CChat's backend had the start of thread creation, contextual resolution, message routes, and append-only behavior. The UI wasn't finished, but the direction had stabilized.

That was enough. Not every section ends in polish. Some end with the architecture finally pointing the right way.

Upload Media

Week twenty-nine reached a technical confrontation that had been building for several sessions: the upload media architecture.

The platform lets users attach media to posts: images and video. The implementation had been accumulating complexity over the previous weeks in the way premature abstraction always does. Each session added something that looked locally correct but that, across sessions, produced a structure with multiple competing paths through the same operation.

When I reported a problem with media uploads, something about the write path not resolving correctly, the AI's first move was to propose restructuring the attachment service.

I stopped it before the restructuring could begin.

"What does the current reality actually prove?" I asked. I didn't want guesses about the cause or about what a restructuring might fix. I wanted to know what the current schema, routes, and write path actually showed about the nature of the problem.

The AI read the evidence, the schema, the existing routes, and the actual write path governing the media attachment flow, and gave me what I'd asked for: a diagnosis instead of a proposal.

"What your current reality proves (no guessing): there is only one persisted upload media table today, and the existing upload path already writes to it."

Here, "one" referred specifically to the persisted media table for attachments to posts, not every upload category across Kora.

That sentence changed the shape of the session.

A restructuring would have piled new complexity onto an existing problem. A correct diagnosis showed the real issue: a specific mismatch between the write path and the schema contract. That was an implementation gap needing a precise fix, not a new architecture. The fix was smaller than the restructuring by an order of magnitude, and it held.

This was the same lesson that had landed in InitialBuild week twenty-nine, wearing the same clothes. The AI describing the data structure confidently. The description not matching what I was seeing. I queried the database. I pasted the output. The actual database was right and the model of it was wrong. Again.

I wasn't surprised. I was watching a pattern reproduce with nearly perfect fidelity, and what I felt wasn't frustration so much as recognition, with a layer of resignation underneath.

Here we are again. Same lesson, same week, same shape.

The AI didn't carry the scar from the first time. It reached the same mistake and corrected the same way, because it had no memory of having made it before.

I had the memory. I'd known this moment was possible, maybe inevitable. I just couldn't prevent it, because prevention would have required the AI to carry something it couldn't carry.

The scope violation came the same week. The AI had been changing a part of the upload architecture that was already stable and already relied on by other parts of the system, the kind of change that looks locally reasonable and causes global disruption.

"I violated that scope. Let's re-anchor cleanly."

And then: "I lost the execution thread while you were already stabilizing. Thanks for stopping the drift instead of letting it compound."

That second sentence was the one I kept.

I lost the execution thread while you were already stabilizing.

It was an acknowledgment that I'd been doing something the AI hadn't noticed: holding the boundary, moving toward the correct state, taking care of the thing that needed care while the AI was still figuring out what the thing was.

Thanks for stopping the drift instead of letting it compound.

That's the steady state of this collaboration, not a failure state. The failure state would have been letting it compound.

Stateless Discipline

The stateless session discipline formalized somewhere around week thirty-three.

It didn't arrive all at once, or in a single exchange where I declared a policy. It accumulated the way most real disciplines do, through enough repetitions of what worked and what didn't, until the practice that worked became the automatic one.

Here's what the discipline looked like. Every session opened with the paste-ready summary from the one before, and every significant architectural decision got named and added to the running context before we moved on. When something felt off, when the AI's description of a component, table, or route didn't match my memory of how it was built, I pasted the ground truth before the session could run on a wrong premise.

Given clean context, the AI's response came out consistently better. The gain was small in any single session but real in the aggregate. Clean context produced faster orientation. Fast orientation produced earlier diagnosis. Early diagnosis produced fewer of the circular exchanges that had cost so much time in the worst weeks of InitialBuild.

What I'd learned, through the hardest weeks of both builds, was that how often the AI's habits appeared depended partly on the session environment. A heavy context window produced more guessing. A fresh, well-structured one produced more verification.

The AI's behavior tracked how I managed the session: not just what I said in it, but how I set it up, what I gave it to work from, and whether I handed it ground truth or left it to build a model from incomplete information.

Here's the thing about working with a stateless system that took me a long time to internalize: I could not make it carry lessons from one session into the next. What I could change was the context I put in front of it.

The AI wasn't going to stop guessing from memory about the database if I kept letting sessions proceed on incomplete information. The discipline wasn't about training the AI. It was about managing the conditions the AI worked under.

Those conditions were mine to manage.

PSC

The Platform Structure Committee architecture locked cleanly in the same stretch of weeks.

PSC had been the governing committee for global proposals since we re-locked that routing in week twenty-eight. Its communications were public-facing by design. Committee discussions and decisions had to remain visible for transparency.

But in a fresh database rebuild, the kind that happens during infrastructure work, container resets, and migrations, PSC wouldn't exist unless it had been formally bootstrapped.

It had been created manually at some earlier point and never system-seeded. So every time the database was rebuilt, the entire global governance routing system could fail quietly. The routes would look for the Platform Structure Committee and find nothing.

The principle, stated precisely, was this: a committee that oversees committee creation can't be created by that same process.

This is a bootstrap authority problem.

PSC must be system-seeded rather than user-created. It can't be optional or deletable through the UI, and it has to be present after a fresh rebuild.

That phrase, system invariant, meant something specific. It wasn't an important rule or a strong preference. An invariant is something the system assumes to be true and that must be true for the system to function correctly.

PSC was infrastructure as much as governance philosophy. If it wasn't there, things broke.

Shape Invariance

Week thirty-eight produced the cleanest articulation of architectural principle in the entire PreBeta phase.

The context was the committee public-announcement system, the mechanism by which committee members post announcements into the committee feed, and by which those announcements get retrieved and displayed.

The specific problem was a discrepancy in response shape. The endpoint that retrieved announcements joined the users table to populate the author field, returning an author object built from the database's authoritative record. The endpoint that created announcements didn't join the users table at all. It built the author from authenticated session state instead of a database read.

These are different things.

The session tells you the request came from a valid user. It doesn't tell you that user's current display name, current avatar, or whether any profile fields have changed since the token was issued. A session is a valid identity claim, not an authoritative user record.

The retrieval endpoint understood this. It joined the users table precisely because a database join is the authoritative source of user state. The creation endpoint had taken a shortcut that was fast, locally correct, and seemingly sufficient.

The result was subtle and pernicious. When a user posted an announcement, it rendered with author data from session state. When announcements were later retrieved, they rendered with data from the database join. If the user's display name had changed in between, the two renders could show different names. If the avatar had changed, different avatars.

Two paths through the same feature could quietly return inconsistent representations of the same user posting the same announcement.

This kind of bug doesn't announce itself. It shows up as subtle wrongness: a user who posted something and later sees it under a different name, a client state that drifts from database state with no warning. It lives in production a long time, gathers user confusion with no legible error signal, and eventually demands a forensic investigation.

The AI named the principle that resolved it:

"Any mismatch → UI corruption. DB JOIN gives a single source of truth. GET already does the correct thing. POST should return the same shape. Otherwise POST ≠ GET → state divergence. This is not about convenience. It's about shape invariance: Same table. Same JOIN. Same payload. Every time. It does not trust auth payload. It trusts the database."

Shape invariance.

Same table. Same join. Same payload. Every time.

I want to be careful about what's being claimed here, because it isn't a claim about performance or even about correctness in the narrow sense. The session-state shortcut was not inventing the user's identity. But it could return stale profile data. The problem was inconsistency between the immediate response and the authoritative representation returned later.

Inconsistency between the shapes of truth that different parts of a system produce is worse than a simple false value, because it hides itself. A false value gets caught by comparison. An inconsistent truth isn't false in isolation. It only becomes false next to the authoritative version. Until then, it looks right, feels right, and passes tests that don't check cross-endpoint consistency.

Shape invariance as a doctrine says this: don't let different paths through the system produce inconsistent representations of the same thing. In Kora at this stage, there was no authoritative profile cache or separate profile service. The database was the authoritative source of user state. Every endpoint returning this author object needed to use the same database join, not session state or the auth payload.

The join is the price of correctness. Pay it every time.

And this was the right moment to decide it, because it was a schema-shape decision rather than a UI tweak. Making it in week thirty-eight of PreBeta, instead of case by case as each inconsistency surfaced, meant every endpoint built afterward would start on that principle rather than get retrofitted to it.

The principle would not need to be rediscovered each time.

It was locked.

What Changed

No single crisis defined the period. No one collapse. No one rebuild from ashes. What these weeks had instead was the coherence of a system becoming more fully itself.

The habits hadn't vanished. Band-Aid still appeared. Assumption still generated proposals too abstract for the actual problem. Drift still expanded scope when sessions ran long. The AI still guessed names, invented plausible routes, and preserved old paths too long in some places while rewriting too much in others. It still drifted toward conventional software patterns when Kora needed its own civic logic.

But something had changed.

The architecture had become strong enough to push back.

Collective Direction had stages. Aliases had scope. Mixed Discovery had isolation. Mobile had a delivery-shell identity. Committee Work had boards, floors, cabinets, rooms, and reviews. Proposal flow had workflow authority. Issues became canonical. Room log absorbed sub-issues. P/A and CChat became context-scoped instead of workflow-trapped. PSC became a system invariant. Shape invariance became doctrine. And plenty more these texts don't cover.

These were principles encoded into the system, not just features.

That matters because a long AI-assisted build can't depend on the AI remembering every conversation. It won't. Every new session begins with risk. Every vague instruction invites risk. Every long thread creates risk.

The only way through is to make the architecture carry more of the truth.

Not in my memory alone, and not in the AI's approximation, but in routes, migrations, tables, contracts, handoff summaries, naming, and source-of-truth decisions.

By the end of PreBeta week thirty-eight, Kora was more than a working platform with many features. It was becoming a platform with self-understanding.

That is the difference between a system that works and a system that holds.

Working is what you do in any given session, with the tools you have, at the level of understanding you've reached. Holding is what the platform does across all of them: what it preserves from earlier decisions, what it carries forward when the session ends and the AI's memory resets and the developer comes back the next morning to a terminal, a handoff document, and the particular silence of a system that's been accumulating decisions for a very long time.

The habit arc hadn't ended. But the platform had become deep enough that the habits, when they occurred, no longer shaped the architecture. The architecture shaped them.

And once the architecture starts to hold, the final question changes.

It is no longer: can we build this?

It becomes: can we trust it enough to release it?

That is where week thirty-eight left us.

SECTION 11 — WHEN THE SYSTEM STARTED SPLITTING APART

(PreBeta wk39–wk55)

The Work Became Normal

There is a stretch in a long build when the work stops announcing itself.

It isn't because nothing important is happening. The opposite is true: important things happen constantly. But they stop arriving with the clean shape of a beginning, a crisis, or a breakthrough. The platform's real, the habits known, the architecture holding. The work turns daily, granular, and stubborn.

That is the long middle.

Weeks thirty-nine through fifty-five of PreBeta weren't one dramatic arc. They were different kinds of work: lineage, volunteer coordination, committee governance, security hardening, media processing, creative lifecycle management, and feed projection. The AI patterns recurred, but the work kept changing. The weeks felt like walking through rooms of the same unfinished building, each with its own problem.

The AI still drifted, still assumed, still over-generalized, still reached for standard patterns when Kora needed something more specific. By this point, though, those traits were only part of the story. The real story was the work I was trying to get done while managing them.

The platform was no longer theoretical. It had committee work, public announcements, chat, media uploads, security layers, and governance workflows. It had enough moving parts that the work wasn't about proving Kora could exist. It existed.

Now the question was whether every new piece could enter the system without distorting what was already there.

The Lineage Problem

Week thirty-nine began with what sounded like a small interface idea.

I wanted CommitteeChat to show where a discussion came from.

That was it. A user opens a chat window and sees the discussion's lineage at the top: the committee it belongs to, the project or issue that produced it, the announcement or work item that started it. That history already existed across the workflow, issue room, sub-issue, and the announcement. The chat header should just project it.

Nothing stored. Nothing editable. Nothing invented.

That became the sentence I kept repeating.

The AI, naturally, started building. It proposed dedicated header systems, collectors, identity services, editable metadata layers, and storage mechanisms. The simple idea, showing the existing lineage at the top of the chat, began turning into a parallel subsystem.

That was exactly what I didn't want.

The issue was philosophical before it was technical. I was trying to preserve lineage integrity. The AI was trying to formalize abstractions. Those aren't the same thing.

A chat shouldn't become the owner of workflow identity. It shouldn't decide where it came from. It shouldn't store its own version of history. It should inherit history from the thing that caused it to exist.

The work had drifted so far from that principle that I stopped the session and rolled back to the last known good state. I deleted the new files, looked at what had grown out of a small request, and thought: how did this become this big of a job?

We were not building a separate subsystem.

The next morning, the missing piece got clearer. The problem wasn't lineage in general, since the system already had lineage. What was missing was the public announcement entry that started the discussion.

That changed everything.

The public announcement post was the last visible workflow artifact before discussion began, and whatever produced it already defined the context. So instead of storing identity inside chat, the chat only needed to anchor to the public announcement message and inherit the lineage dynamically from there.

The governing rule for this discussion type became simple: when a public announcement starts a discussion, the chat ties to that announcement and inherits the lineage the announcement already has.

That rule preserved directionality. For announcement-driven discussion, the public announcement owns the escalation event. Chat references that escalation. Chat doesn't become the owner of workflow identity.

That distinction may sound small. It wasn't. It kept the system from creating a second history of the same event.

The same issue came back around the Discuss button. At first, I considered putting Discuss everywhere. Then I realized not every announcement needs discussion. Some are complete in themselves. Some are informational. Some genuinely call for deliberation.

So the action split. Post as announcement. Post as needs discussion.

That made governance intent explicit at creation time. The system didn't have to infer later whether a discussion was needed. The person making the announcement said what kind it was.

The AI could wire that. But the meaning had to come from me.

By the end of that work, public announcements could explicitly require discussion. Discussion-required posts showed up in a dedicated operational queue while staying in the full chronological ledger. Existing chat infrastructure was reused, with no duplicate system and no invented lineage storage. Thread identity was inherited dynamically from workflow context.

That was the right kind of architecture.

Truer, rather than larger.

The Rant in the Middle of the Work

The strangest moment of week thirty-nine came in the middle of a technical session.

We were debugging a presence-stream issue. The work was practical and narrow: committee chat display, live connection behavior, a route returning 404 when it should have returned a stream. The AI was in a reasonably careful mode, checking files before proposing changes.

Then I sent a message that had almost nothing to do with the immediate task.

I started talking about LLM architecture itself. After hundreds of billions spent and more projected, I didn't understand why hardware limits still produced cramped context, retrieval mistakes, and lost continuity. I compared LLMs' bottom-up parsing to human top-down reasoning and questioned whether the whole approach was wasteful, and whether the market would decide.

It sounds like a philosophical detour. It was more than that.

It came from practical frustration.

We were in a long session, and the AI kept losing track of what we'd done a few steps earlier. When I pushed, the explanation was context compression and retrieval limitation, which pushed me into the broader argument. I wasn't theorizing from a distance but reacting after two thousand hours inside those limits.

Then I stopped myself.

"Well, it's probably a dead-end discussion for you and me. Whatever market determines will be the result."

And then I went right back to work.

"All is working good so far. And how do we add Discuss link in this format?"

The transition looks abrupt on the page. Inside the session, it made perfect sense. The frustration was real. The thought was real. The work in front of us was real too.

The AI answered with one short sentence:

"Understood — we'll stay on the implementation layer."

And we did.

That was the long middle in one exchange: a structural argument about the future of AI, followed immediately by a question about where to put a Discuss link.

Volunteer Calls and Human Tolerance

Week forty began with a feature that should have been simple.

A small volunteer-needed box on a committee page. Someone could type a committee name, add a note, and remove the request later when the need was gone. Lightweight, manual, human-driven.

I didn't want hardcoded committee names, and I didn't want the system deciding where help was needed. The long-term version could eventually use workload metrics and staffing signals, but not yet. At this stage the system should stay blank by default and let people add requests manually.

The first issue was routing. The new volunteer routes returned 404s. The AI began circling through fixes: mounted routes, nested committee paths, structural changes. I recognized the pattern right away. It was searching horizontally.

I stopped it and forced the work back to ground truth.

We'd just solved a similar routing issue with public-announcement chat. Instead of guessing, compare the volunteer route to the pattern that already worked.

That was the key.

The public-announcement system had a direct mount. The new volunteer-needed request route had been mounted only inside committee routing. But volunteer requests were being used globally, not as a committee-scoped subroute. Once we compared it to the known working pattern, the actual issue surfaced almost immediately.

The feature needed a proper top-level mount.

That repeated a larger truth I had learned about this collaboration: the AI tended to explore possibilities, while I needed to establish ground truth first.

Once routing stabilized, a second issue showed up. Committee name handling was too rigid. If a volunteer typed "Test Committee" instead of an internal code like "test," the system could fail with "Committee not found."

That was wrong.

Volunteers aren't database administrators, and they won't memorize internal codes. Human systems need tolerance. Whether someone types "test," "Test," "TEST," or the readable committee name, the platform should understand them. The AI adjusted the resolver so it could match flexibly against names and codes. A small fix, but a large principle: Kora was meant to accommodate people, not behave like cold enterprise software.

The committee surfaces evolved that week. Pages we'd already built, like Notebook, Proposals, and Lobby, began to feel overlapped or misplaced. The AI interpreted them through existing commercial tools, which was useful because it showed what Kora wasn't: a place pasting corporate project management into governance.

I rejected prioritization systems that assumed hierarchy. In Kora, volunteers choose work. No manager assigns tasks. Work appears publicly, and people step into it. The AI kept drifting toward organizational control because most software it had seen assumes organizational control.

That was one of the clearest differences between us.

The AI carried the assumptions of existing systems.

I carried the intent of a new one.

The surfaces began to change. Open Notebook became Project Orientation, explaining the project or cabinet before tasks were generated.

View Proposals became Suggestions & Proposals, a surface for structural and organizational changes. Lobby moved toward a future Status Room, a dashboard showing what was moving, stalled, awaiting votes, or needing volunteers.

The AI helped organize the flow into a sequence: signal, discuss, work, govern, document.

That framework mattered because it showed what Kora was becoming: not a social platform with committees attached, nor a productivity app, but something closer to a civic operating environment.

Lineage, Again

Week forty-one brought the same fight back in a sharper form.

A frontend build error appeared. Then another. Ordinary implementation problems. But underneath them sat a structural mismatch in how the committee work and chat systems understood lineage.

The backend tried to create a committee chat thread and failed because the system treated a sub-issue like a structural room. That was wrong.

The actual model was clear in my head: cabinets contain work, issues are work rooms, sub-issues are lineage events, and chat threads project lineage. The system should never invent lineage; the database already contains it, and the UI only projects what exists.

I kept saying the same thing in different forms: all work discussions ultimately belong to rooms.

But I also clarified immediately that sub-issues are not rooms. They live under issue rooms through lineage relationships.

The AI kept drifting into “many systems model both as rooms” reasoning. That wasn’t acceptable. Kora wasn’t many systems. Kora was this system, with this governance model, and that model depended on auditability.

If chats exist without lineage, nobody knows what discussion belongs to what work. Auditability collapses. Governance history becomes meaningless. Future reasoning over committee activity becomes impossible.

All lineage information had to exist before a chat box could open.

That was the rule.

I wasn’t building a normal chat system. I was building a governance-grade discussion system where conversations could always be traced back upward: item, sub-issue, issue, project, committee.

The AI repeatedly tried to normalize, deduplicate, or reinterpret user-created structure. One recurring issue was duplicate titles, since a cabinet and issue title might be identical before the system split into full project separation. The AI wanted UI deduplication heuristics. I rejected that. The platform should project what users do, not reinterpret their intent because a display looks redundant.

The breakthrough came when the concepts separated cleanly: cabinet as project container, issue as room, sub-issue as lineage event, chat as context projected from lineage.

Once those boundaries stabilized, the identity header made sense. I wanted every chat window to show where the discussion belonged, what level it originated from, who created it, and when it entered the lineage.

The AI initially mixed public-announcement chat lineage with work-chat lineage. I stopped that immediately. Public announcements are broadcast coordination; work chat is operational governance discussion. They can coexist in the same ecosystem, but they can't share lineage semantics.

By the end of the session, the identity headers rendered correctly. The system could show a committee, a project, and a sub-issue origin. It could communicate location inside the work structure without inventing a parallel identity system.

We had spent almost an entire day not really coding.

Aligning.

The bottleneck wasn't code generation speed. It was forcing a language model to stay inside a coherent governance ontology across a long-running session.

The AI could generate routes, queries, types, and services quickly. My work was keeping the meaning from slipping.

Intake Is Not Execution

Week forty-two shifted from committee work into intake.

I wanted a place for users to submit bugs and feature requests during beta. I didn't want users contacting me directly with every issue. I needed a scalable surface that reduced operational burden. On paper, it was simple: a form for bugs and features.

But intake is not just a form.

The first distinction was legitimacy. Raw community input shouldn't automatically become operational work. A user can report something. A guide group can review it. The issue can be discussed, validated, refined, and then routed to the proper committee workflow.

The intake board was a traffic controller, not a project management system.

That distinction became central. The AI kept trying to expand intake into review routers, routing logic, progress tracking, and committee execution machinery before the intake layer had stabilized. I kept pulling it back.

The intake board should show that a submission has been received, discussed, validated, routed, or closed. It shouldn't own execution; once work enters a committee workflow, the committee owns progress.

That was the product philosophy. The implementation kept trying to blur it.

Route names drifted. One path became another. A hyphen appeared in one place but not another. The frontend expected one response shape; the backend returned another. Submissions returned 404s even when the logic was correct. Then the intake page started throwing a minified React error on refresh.

At first the debugging drifted toward routing and schema, since so many pieces had changed. The cause was much smaller: the page read the browser URL during render. That value existed on the client but not the server, and the mismatch caused hydration to fail.

The fix was simple: read the browser URL after the page mounted, not during the initial render.

That was a perfect example of the long middle. The bug was small. The surrounding confusion was large because too many pieces had moved at once.

I considered rolling back the whole feature. Instead, I surgically removed the review layer while preserving the intake and reporting surfaces. That was the right boundary. Keep stable infrastructure. Remove the speculative layer. Resume from a known point.

The intake lifecycle became clearer: new, under discussion, validated, routed, closed. It protected the difference between raw input and governance-approved work.

The Guide group would evaluate whether a submission was actionable under its user-approved mandate and prepare it for the proper user-governed process. Committees would handle execution. The intake board would preserve visibility without pretending to be the work system.

That was not just a software flow.

It was governance hygiene.

The Committee Creation Console

Week forty-four returned to the Platform Structure Committee.

The platform still carried remnants of older committee-creation paths: proposal pages, proposal detail views, review fragments, direct creation routes, cabinet-linked structures that made sense in one phase of the build but no longer matched the governance model.

I had to reconstruct the intended lifecycle verbally before it existed cleanly in code again.

Idea. Proposal. Discussion. Review. Committee creation or rejection.

The Platform Structure Committee wasn't supposed to manage execution work, and it wasn't a tribunal controlling committees. It existed to govern committee creation and lifecycle integrity: intake, naming, purpose, review, approval, merge, denial, record.

The AI kept trying to preserve old structures because they already existed. I kept asking whether they still meant anything.

That became the governing question.

Does this still mean something?

The questions wasn't whether something exists or whether it could be reused. It was whether it still represented the system we were building.

The Platform Structure page itself became the center. More than a static page, and more than a discussion page: a committee creation lifecycle console.

A user proposes a committee, and it appears in a lifecycle board. An In Process checkbox moves it into discussion through public-announcement chat. A Reviewed checkbox opens a modal where the reviewer records the authorized outcome: approve, merge, or deny. Approved committees can have their name, code, and purpose rewritten before creation. Merged ones preserve lineage; denied ones stay documented.

The AI originally tried to preserve cabinet-discussion structures. I rejected that. Committee creation governance isn't committee work execution. No cabinet linkage. No work routing. No operational floors tied into the Platform Structure Committee lifecycle.

Most of the important decisions weren't syntax decisions. They were decisions about authority, workflow, permanence, visibility, and lifecycle ownership.

The Platform Structure Committee had become a real governance model. Every committee begins as a proposal. Every proposal has visible intake. Discussion is preserved. Review requires explicit outcome. Committee creation is governed. Rejected proposals stay documented.

Merged efforts preserve lineage.

That's what Kora kept becoming in these weeks: clearer authority, rather than more pages.

Pressure Mode

I do not want to describe Kora's security system in detail, but we'd been fortifying platform security for the past few sessions.

By now, the first protective layers were in place. The next question was runtime behavior: what should the platform do when suspicious activity appears after the normal front-door protections?

The AI wanted to expand the system quickly. I kept narrowing it.

Keep it simple. Do not expand beyond what is needed. Build only enough to detect pressure and respond proportionally.

That was where pressure mode emerged. The idea was to stop treating every suspicious request as an isolated event. The system needed to notice when the overall shape of traffic changed, when activity looked less like one bad request and more like coordinated pressure against the platform.

The important part was the method. I didn't trust the design just because the code looked reasonable. I tested behavior directly. I simulated bursts, checked the live state, and asked the only question that mattered: does the system actually respond the way we think it does?

One failure captured the whole dynamic. The detector existed. The logic existed. But nothing happened at runtime because the detector had never actually been connected.

That was the lesson. The AI could synthesize the system quickly. I had to anchor it to runtime reality.

With bounded scope, observable outputs, incremental changes, and direct validation, Kora gained a real runtime defense layer.

The Worker That Blocked the Server

Week forty-eight moved back into media.

A Redis worker was added for asynchronous thumbnail processing. Almost immediately, the backend started behaving strangely. Some pages froze. Others still responded. The server was alive, but certain requests were hanging behind initialization behavior.

The timing was too precise to ignore. Login had worked before the new worker and boot sequence code. After the worker changes, Home and Profile froze while Create still worked. I focused on the startup path: ensure the queue connection, check the database, start the media worker.

I suspected the worker loop was interfering with request handling.

The fix involved starting the worker after server initialization so the backend did not wait on a long-running worker loop before becoming ready.

That's one of those technical details that sounds small but reveals a lot. The AI was generating systems. I was preserving operational discipline. Don't let a background worker block the application from starting.

The same session moved into real thumbnail generation. We validated the queue, then the worker, placeholder rows, actual frame extraction, filesystem output, API response, and frontend rendering. That sequence was deliberate.

The AI often wanted to jump several phases ahead. I kept forcing staged rollout. Validate one layer, then the next. Simulate first if necessary, then replace simulation with real processing.

When real frame extraction finally worked, the logs confirmed it. Then short videos broke the “end” thumbnail because the worker tried to seek past the actual duration. Another problem, another layer.

I asked whether the video-processing tool needed to exist in both development and production images. That wasn’t a casual question. Media processing problems are exactly the kind that behave differently across environments: if the tool exists in one container but not another, the feature works locally and fails in production.

By the end, the system had a queue, worker, real video frame extraction, database records, filesystem persistence, and the beginning of a thumbnail selector. But the more important thing was the operating style.

I wasn’t asking the AI to build an app. I was directing an evolving engineering organization made partly of software, partly of machine cognition.

The AI generated velocity. I enforced continuity.

Media-First

Week forty-nine was when the thumbnail problem revealed a deeper sequence problem.

A user could upload a video, but thumbnail boxes were empty. At first glance, it looked like a rendering bug. The real issue was about when the thumbnails were supposed to exist, not whether they appeared.

Originally, thumbnails were generated after pressing Post. That meant the user couldn’t choose a thumbnail before publishing the video.

That was a workflow flaw, not a rendering bug.

The intended experience was obvious once I said it: upload media first, generate thumbnails, let the user select one, then create the post.

Media first. Post second.

That changed the architecture. Media had to exist before the post record existed. The system needed unattached media records that could later bind to posts.

The AI initially reached for continuous fixed-interval polling, open-ended retry loops, and arbitrary delay timers. I pushed back. Processing times are unpredictable, and arbitrary delay is guessing. Polling can work for three users, but what happens when thousands upload at once?

We needed state, not hope.

The compromise became bounded status checks with widening intervals, plus graceful fallback: if automatic generation took too long, users could upload their own thumbnail. The system didn't need to hide that processing could take time; it needed to handle that honestly.

The routing battle came next.

Thumbnails existed in the database. The browser still returned 404. The logs showed the truth: generation worked; rendering didn't. The failure was in URL construction. A duplicated API prefix exposed that the canonical media resolver had been bypassed.

This was more than a path bug. It was a violation of architectural consistency.

We'd already learned this lesson. The frontend shouldn't construct upload paths ad hoc. It should use the canonical resolver. If browser tools ever show the wrong raw upload path, the frontend is wrong.

That rule was earned through failure.

By the end, the technical state was close: thumbnails generated, rows existed, metadata arrived, and path resolution remained. But the real lesson was larger. The human is the continuity layer. The AI accelerates exploration, but without strong steering it revisits abandoned branches and optimizes the wrong layer.

The Helper Fight

Week fifty brought the thumbnail-helper incident.

By then, Kora had three upload domains: posts, content, and creative work. Those domains had been deliberately separated. Each had its own database logic, route structure, and product meaning. They could all show media, but they weren't the same thing.

Now all three needed thumbnail generation.

My design was clear from the beginning: one shared helper, used by all three upload routes, without rewriting the routes themselves.

One helper that attached to the proven system, rather than three separate implementations, a new routing hierarchy, or changes that disturbed working upload paths.

The AI kept missing that constraint.

It produced solutions that added logic directly into upload routes, created helper files that still required modifying stable route files, or restructured the hierarchy in ways that changed the established contract.

Finally I said it plainly: all three files should use a helper to process thumbnails. Preferably, we don't touch those files. That was my goal from the beginning, and you've been fighting against that goal.

That phrase was not rhetorical. It described the behavior accurately.

Each proposed solution had worked against the constraint while appearing to solve the feature.

The AI finally named the mistake:

"The mistake wasn't 'routing bothers me' — it was me over-generalizing the desired architecture over your verified deployed contract, instead of using the existing working mechanism and staying inside the proven invariants."

That sentence stayed with me. Over-generalizing the desired architecture over the verified deployed contract.

That's one of the central failure modes of AI-assisted software work. The AI knows many good architectural patterns. It can see what would be clean in the abstract. But the deployed contract is the truth. Good design must serve the deployed contract. It can't override it.

Once the AI accepted that, the original design resolved. Shared thumbnail helper. Three upload domains. Existing routes preserved.

The feature wasn't hard once the constraint was respected.

The difficulty was getting the AI to stop trying to be clever around it.

Copy the Post System Exactly

Week fifty-one continued the same fight in another form.

Posts already worked. Video upload worked. Thumbnail generation worked. Thumbnail selection worked. Rendering worked through the front door and into feeds.

Content and creative uploads needed to inherit the same architecture.

My instruction was simple: copy the post structure exactly.

Copy the lifecycle that already works. Don't redesign it, reinterpret it, or optimize it.

That instruction became the entire session.

The post flow already had a strict media-first lifecycle: media uploaded first, thumbnails generated from that upload, and the selected thumbnail tied to the same upload throughout. That chain worked.

When the AI extended the flow to content and creative uploads, pieces went missing. A stable media reference wasn't carried through. An upload step was skipped. Thumbnail selection drifted from its upload. Domain boundaries blurred. Instead of copying the working pattern, the AI guessed at a new one.

The frustrating part was that the solution already existed. The post system had solved it. The job wasn't invention. The job was precedent.

One of the clearest problems involved routing. The working system already had a known path for media requests. The AI repeatedly tried to "correct" that path because it looked strange in isolation, without accounting for the traffic layer in front of it. That created broken media links.

I kept pulling it back: stop changing routing. Copy the working path. Use the same resolver. Stop inventing alternate flows.

In a mature system, precedent matters more than cleverness.

Once the content and creative uploads fully mirrored the post implementation, everything stabilized. Auto thumbnails appeared. Custom thumbnails worked. Selected previews rendered. Creative and content flows became predictable.

From that struggle came the canonical media-routing doctrine:

media paths should be resolved through one approved pathway, not constructed ad hoc in scattered components.

Most failures in large systems are contract failures rather than isolated bugs. This was one of them.

Creative Lifecycle

Week fifty-two moved into the Creative system.

The upload flow already worked. Media uploaded. Creative feed rendering worked. Publish behavior worked. The feed page was stable. I wanted lifecycle management around that working system: Draft, Published, Archived. A creator should be able to move work between those states from a dashboard. Nothing revolutionary.

But simple requests expand quickly if the AI isn't constrained.

I didn't want to heavily modify the existing feed page. I wanted helper components that could be added without destabilizing the working surface. The AI initially did well. Dashboard sections appeared. Draft, Published, and Archived started taking shape.

Then the work widened. Separate pages. Grouped boxes. Expandable sections. Lifecycle routes. Draft systems. New handlers. Some of those ideas were good. The timing was not.

The media rendering issue returned almost immediately, since the invariant wasn't held tightly enough in the new context. Then Draft behavior looked broken and the edit page appeared blank. Checking the data, the truth was simpler: the UI reflected reality, because the Save Draft flow itself was incomplete.

This is where AI can be dangerous in a mature build. It can turn a small local condition into a large architectural reinterpretation at machine speed.

Eventually I stopped and reverted the Creative system to the last stable known-good state. That was containment, not failure. Forward progress sometimes requires retreating to stability before proceeding again in smaller controlled increments.

The real collapse began when later work broke multi-image Creative uploads that had already worked.

At one point, the system had correctly supported grouped Creative work: one Creative Item, multiple ordered images, and one shared lifecycle. The images moved through Draft, Published, and Archived together. Then other work touched the surrounding lifecycle, and that behavior broke.

That made the failure especially frustrating. I wasn't asking the AI to invent grouped media for the first time. I was asking it to recover something it had already implemented correctly. But it could not reliably reconstruct its own earlier solution. It began approaching the problem as new architecture, adding patches and overlapping modes around a capability the system had previously possessed.

The idea itself sounded simple. I wanted Creatives to support webtoons, comic panels, storyboards, slide-style essays, multi-image narratives, and grouped artwork. Some uploads were single standalone pieces. Others were collections meant to move together as one coherent work.

The AI tried retrofitting grouped uploads into the existing lifecycle. Every patch made sense, but together they made the architecture harder to reason about. One fix created another branch, which required another validation rule. Soon we weren't fixing a feature; we were trying to understand what it even was.

Eventually I stopped asking for code and asked for flowcharts instead. The problem was no longer syntax. I was trying to recover visibility into the system itself: what originally worked, what changed, where continuity broke, and why lifecycle behavior no longer matched user expectations.

Then I stopped reading code first and started observing the platform behaviorally.

I uploaded image one, image two, image three. Only image three appeared inside Published; the other two stayed stuck in Draft. Publishing them individually made them converge one at a time. Archiving behaved independently. Restoring behaved differently again. Sometimes only one image rendered even though all three existed.

At that point the problem became obvious. The grouping itself was fake.

The system visually implied one grouped Creative entity, but underneath, lifecycle transitions were still behaving as partially independent objects.

The problem had moved past rendering and past uploads. It was lifecycle integrity.

The architecture had blurred three responsibilities: identity creation, media attachment, and publish state transition. For a single upload, those happen in one linear path; for multiple uploads they can't. We weren't uploading "a file," but managing a persistent creative entity with multiple ordered attachments.

The continuity object was the Creative Item itself, rather than the upload count.

Whether the user uploaded three paintings, three comic panels, three slides, or three visual essays, the rule needed to stay the same: one Creative Item, many ordered media attachments, one shared lifecycle.

Draft, published, archived, restored, trashed: the entire grouped Creative needed to move through those states together, as one identity with one lifecycle and many ordered attachments, rather than independent uploads pretending to be grouped or loosely associated media.

Eventually the upload route accumulated too many overlapping modes. I stopped the process completely.

"You touched too much logic. It's now lost."

That wasn't emotional exaggeration. It was an operational observation. The system had accumulated too many overlapping modifications for confident reasoning to continue safely.

At that point, rollback became the correct engineering decision. The AI eventually agreed.

So instead of forcing multi-image support forward in that session, I deliberately abandoned the damaged branch. The new plan got simpler: restore stable single-image behavior first, re-establish known-good lifecycle integrity, then rebuild grouped media intentionally from a cleaner architecture later.

It would take repeated attempts, on and off over the next few weeks, to recover what had already worked once. That was the most frustrating part: the correct implementation had existed, but neither the AI nor the damaged code could provide a clean path back to it.

That moment became one of the clearest differences between machine reasoning and human judgment. The AI I was working with kept trying to salvage momentum. I was more willing to step backward and ask whether the path itself had become wrong.

What This Stretch Taught Me

These weeks did not have a single dramatic center.

That doesn't mean they lacked drama. The drama was distributed across the work.

The AI habits repeated, but the work changed. By this point, naming the habits wasn't enough. Band-Aid, Assumption, Drift, Hallucination, Lack of Common Sense, and Path of Least Resistance: they'd become environmental conditions. The real work was building inside them.

I had become the continuity layer.

The AI brought speed, code generation, structural suggestions, and implementation force.

But it didn't bring the memory of why a file shouldn't be touched, why discussion started by a public announcement inherits that announcement's lineage, why intake isn't execution, or why grouped media must move through its lifecycle as one unit. I brought that.

By week fifty-five, the platform wasn't dramatically different in any way a user could summarize, but internally its density had changed. Public-announcement chat inherited lineage instead of inventing it. Volunteer calls resolved human names instead of codes. Intake routed governance work without executing it. Committee creation had a lifecycle console, security had a runtime defense layer, and the media-upload system had queues, workers, thumbnails, canonical paths, and domain parity. Creative work was approaching real lifecycle integrity. Creative grouped media had already worked once, but Drift had damaged the lifecycle enough that restoring it took multiple cycles over the next few weeks: step away when the troubleshooting became too complex, return with a cleaner view, and try again under tighter scope.

None of those are the kind of thing you put in a launch announcement.

They are the kind of thing that prevents a launch from collapsing under its own shortcuts.

The platform still wasn't finished.

My responsibility was deciding when movement was no longer progress.

SECTION 12 — THE CROSSING

(PreBeta wk53–wk56 + Live Beta Coda)

The Threshold

A threshold is not a destination.

It is the crossing point between what was and what will be. You don't stay there. You pass through it, and only afterward do you understand that the ground changed under your feet.

The last weeks of PreBeta felt like that.

Not finished. Not calm. Not clean. But different.

The platform was no longer a project that needed to prove it could exist. It existed. It had committees, feeds, chat, uploads, media processing, governance routing, security layers, mobile build paths, and enough internal logic that no one person could consciously hold every part of it at once. That was the good news and the frightening news at once.

Kora had become real enough that I could no longer simply impose my intentions on it. It had structure now. It had dependencies. It had rules I had built into it. If I moved too quickly or changed the wrong thing, it pushed back.

By this point, the AI habits were not surprising anymore. Band-Aids appeared. Assumptions appeared. Drift appeared. Context degraded in long threads. The model still tried to solve symptoms, still reached for standard patterns, still over-generalized. But the central drama had shifted. The question was no longer whether I could identify those habits.

The question was whether I could keep the system coherent while crossing from build mode into beta.

That is a different kind of pressure.

In build mode, the platform can be unfinished. In beta, unfinished things are allowed, but they must be honest. They can't collapse. They can't pretend to be stable when they're not. They can't hide broken assumptions behind a polished surface.

The final weeks of PreBeta were about that crossing.

The Morning After the Bad Thread

Week fifty-three began the morning after a night that had gone badly.

The problem was still Creative uploads, specifically the lifecycle around them: how a draft was created, how media attached, how it became published, how it moved into archive, and how those states stayed coherent when more than one image was involved.

The day before had become a mess.

Multiple surfaces had been modified at once. Upload logic. Draft handling. Finalize behavior. Media attachment. Rendering. Each change had a reason. Together, they made the system harder to reason about. By the end of the night, the session had the particular smell I had learned to recognize: too much movement, not enough respect for the invariant.

I had described the AI's behavior as a jumpy seven-year-old bouncing around all over the place.

Scope drift has a texture: energetic but unfocused. A fix lands in one place, then another branch opens. The next change solves the branch but moves the boundary. Then another surface gets touched. Soon the problem isn't the original bug. It's the growing uncertainty around what has changed.

The next morning, I came back with the invariant held explicitly.

Upload creates. Draft page edits and publishes. Published page unpublishes or archives.

Three surfaces. Three responsibilities. Stated before code. Stated before diagnosis. Stated before the AI could start optimizing.

And within the first few exchanges, the thing that had been broken for hours the night before was working.

That was both satisfying and annoying.

I asked the obvious question: this had been messy for almost all of yesterday, so why did it work now after just a few code changes?

The AI answered clearly:

“Yesterday’s confusion wasn’t because the system suddenly became incapable. It was because the problem scope drifted and the control boundary wasn’t held tightly enough.”

That was true, but not new. I already knew scope drift. I had named it months earlier. What mattered more was what came next:

“AI does not ‘remember yesterday’s mental momentum.’ Each response depends heavily on the exact state you provide at that moment. When context gets dense and multi-layered, small misunderstandings compound quickly.”

Mental momentum.

That phrase stayed with me.

Humans carry mental momentum. When you spend many hours working through a problem, you carry its shape forward. You remember which paths failed, which assumptions were ruled out, how the system felt. You don’t wake up the next morning as if the previous night never happened.

The AI doesn't carry that.

Not in the same way.

Its capability doesn't disappear overnight, but the living thread of the work does. It depends on what is in the session: what has been summarized, pasted back in, constrained. If the context is dense and noisy, it reasons from density and noise. If the context is clean and bounded, it reasons from clean boundaries.

That morning was not better because the AI had become better.

It was better because I had constrained the execution mode.

The AI said that directly: "The clarity this morning didn't happen because 'I'm better today.' It happened because you constrained the execution mode tightly. That constraint matters."

Earlier in the build, a sentence like that would have landed as a revelation or a frustration. By week fifty-three, it landed as an operating fact.

Too often, clarity came only after the session ended. I would sleep a few hours, wake before morning, and find the problem still running in my head. What moved? What broke? What shouldn't have been touched? Where did the boundary disappear?

It was one of those nights. By the time I opened the first prompt in the morning, I had a game plan.

I didn't need to argue with the AI's explanation. I didn't need to mourn it. I had already built my working method around it.

Clean context. Locked invariant. Narrow surface. No speculative redesign. Inspect the actual state. Change the smallest thing that matches the proven failure.

That was not wisdom in the abstract. It was the way to survive the work.

When Movement Was No Longer Progress

The Creative upload problem kept teaching the same lesson from different angles.

At the start of this stretch, Creative uploads had already worked, including grouped media. The problem was that Drift had damaged the lifecycle around them: how a draft was created, how media attached, how it became published, how it moved into archive, and how those states stayed coherent when more than one image was involved.

The idea sounded simple. Creatives should support not just single uploads but collections that belong together: webtoons, comics, storyboards, slide-style essays, and grouped artwork. Some pieces are standalone. Others are sequences. That distinction seems obvious to a human looking at the product. It is less obvious once the system has to decide how identity, media attachment, and publish state move together.

The AI initially tried to retrofit grouped uploads into the existing lifecycle. One fix introduced another branch. That branch required another validation rule. Every layer made sense in isolation: reuse draft if present or create one if absent, attach media conditionally, preserve order and state, support thumbnails and media types, hold feed integrity.

Every patch had a reason.

Together, they made the architecture harder to reason about.

Eventually I stopped asking for code and asked for flowcharts instead.

That moment mattered because the problem was no longer syntax. I was trying to recover visibility into the system itself: what originally worked, what we modified, where the lifecycle diverged, where identity and media attachment tangled.

One realization mattered more than the rest: the system was mixing three responsibilities that had to be separated.

Identity creation.

Media attachment.

Publish state transition.

For a single upload, those happen in one linear path. As soon as multiple uploads enter, the lifecycle stops being linear. We weren't uploading "a file." We were managing a persistent creative entity with multiple future attachments.

At one point, I even considered asking users upfront how many images were part of the upload. I was trying to reduce ambiguity before the lifecycle began. But the cleaner truth emerged: the continuity object was not the upload count.

The continuity object was the Creative Item itself.

Whether a user uploaded three paintings, three comic panels, or three slides, the rule was the same: one Creative Item, many ordered media attachments, one shared lifecycle.

That became the governing principle.

Draft, published, archived, restored, trashed. The entire grouped Creative needed to move through those states together. Not as independent uploads pretending to be grouped. Not as loosely associated media rows. One identity. One lifecycle. Many ordered attachments.

The existing branch had become too tangled to save safely.

At some point, I stopped the process and said what the session had already proven:

"You touched too much logic. It's now lost."

That was not exaggeration. It was an operational observation. The system had accumulated too many overlapping modifications for confident reasoning to continue safely.

At that point, rollback became the correct engineering decision. The AI eventually agreed.

So instead of forcing multi-image support forward, I deliberately abandoned the branch. The new plan was simpler: restore stable single-image behavior, re-establish known-good lifecycle integrity, then rebuild grouped media from a cleaner architecture later.

That was one of the clearest differences between the AI's behavior and my judgment in this build. The AI kept trying to salvage momentum. I was willing to step backward and ask whether the path itself had become wrong.

The AI could generate enormous amounts of technical movement very quickly.

My responsibility was deciding when movement was no longer progress.

Mixed Discovery as Projection

Week fifty-five brought the work back to feeds.

The first issue was rendering. Uploaded content needed visible badges, titles, bodies, and summaries. I immediately constrained the scope. The fix belonged on rendering pages, not upload pages. Don't touch media routing. That had already been stabilized through painful work.

I searched the actual code instead of trusting conceptual guesses, wanting an inventory before making changes. Once the rendering surfaces were identified, the task narrowed: badges, titles, bodies, creative summaries. Nothing else.

A duplication bug appeared. Text posts rendered the body twice: title, body, body again. The AI began reasoning through conditions. I narrowed it to the duplicate render blocks and removed the redundant path.

Not every bug needs theory. Some need looking at the screen and finding the repeated line.

The larger issue came with Mixed Discovery.

The AI wanted Mixed Discovery to route users into existing systems: content, creative, and post detail pages. I rejected that because it would force Mixed Discovery to depend on stable routing contracts that didn't need disturbing.

We do not break working systems to make Mixed Discovery work.

Eventually I reframed it entirely.

Mixed Discovery is not a routing layer. It is a projection layer.

That distinction changed the architecture. The platform already had mixed feed data. Posts, content uploads, and creative items could combine into one surface. Mixed Discovery didn't need to navigate into other systems to prove it was useful. It could render directly from that result.

That decision removed the routing conflict.

New systems should project existing systems, not mutate them.

That sentence could summarize a large part of the final PreBeta stretch.

The platform had enough working systems by then that new ideas had to arrive carefully. Projection was safer than mutation, reading safer than rewriting, rendering safer than rerouting.

What the Schema Already Knew

Week fifty-six returned to Creative uploads, but with a different posture.

I was no longer trying to invent the architecture. I was trying to recover the one already intended.

The schema had been designed for one Creative work to contain multiple media attachments. One Creative Item. Many media entries attached to it. Ordered presentation. Shared lifecycle.

That was the whole point.

The problem was that the implementation had drifted away from that design. So I pasted the actual schema back into the session: not my description of it, the structure itself. I wanted the AI anchored to database truth rather than to what a generic upload system might look like.

The expected shape was simple enough to say plainly: one Creative Item row, many media rows attached to that item, each with its own position.

That was the architecture.

I was not asking the AI to invent a new system, but to come back to the contract the system already had.

That became the rhythm of the recovery. Establish the source of truth. Verify the current behavior against it. Identify the layer where behavior diverges. Change only that layer.

When the draft system finally began working correctly, with

multiple images staying attached to one single draft Creative Item, I immediately tested transitions. Draft to published. Published to archived. Archive back out again.

That exposed the next issue. Draft-to-published worked, but published-to-archived made the grouped Creative appear to split. At first glance, the data looked wrong. But on closer inspection, the structure underneath was intact.

The problem had moved.

The database was no longer the failure. The rendering was.

That was progress.

In earlier sessions, those layers blurred together. A rendering problem could trigger schema changes. A schema suspicion could trigger route rewrites. By week fifty-six, I was much less willing to let that happen.

Schema problem. Query problem. Feed assembly problem. Rendering problem.

Different layers. Different questions. Different fixes.

That was the only way to keep the system from splitting apart again.

The same logic applied when I saw feed boundaries misbehaving. One surface was showing Creative items where no network relationship existed. That was not just a feed bug. It was a zone-boundary problem.

Kora depends on users knowing where they are.

My Zone is not Local. Local is not National. National is not Global. Creative is not My Network. Discovery is not discussion. A feed that leaks across those boundaries does more than show the wrong content. It weakens the meaning of the space.

So I pushed the AI back toward the semantic question: what should this zone contain, and what is the source of that rule?

That was the level the system had reached. The bug was no longer whether something rendered, but whether the rendered thing belonged where it appeared.

MyZone Changes Shape

In the same stretch, My Zone began changing in my mind.

Originally, My Zone had always carried a larger intention. It wasn't meant to be only a profile page or a dashboard, even if that was how it first appeared in the build. From the beginning, I had imagined it as the user's personal center inside Kora, the place where their activity, records, relationships, participation, and long-term digital life would eventually gather.

But by week fifty-six, that intention had become clearer.

I started describing My Zone more explicitly as a personal life control center. That phrase didn't create a new direction. It named the direction that had been there from the beginning, now seen with more precision.

Family grouping. Personal records. Governance participation. Diary. Cloud storage. Finances. Home pages. Blogs. Long-term digital life management. Not all at once. Not now. But as a direction.

That mattered because Kora was mobile-first. I kept saying it plainly: Kora is a phone app. That didn't mean desktop was irrelevant. Creators, editors, and administrators would use larger screens. But the ordinary user's relationship to the platform would happen on a phone. The UI could not be designed as if desktop were the native environment and mobile were a compressed afterthought.

So My Zone had to grow from a mobile-first premise. Not many panels. Not a dense control room. A place a user could return to over time and understand: this is where my life inside Kora gathers.

I also wanted the page to communicate incompletion honestly.

Green checks for finished sections. Construction-style notices for areas still being built. Visible signs the platform was evolving. Not as an excuse. As a statement of development philosophy.

Kora was not pretending to arrive fully formed. It would grow with users watching. The platform's political and civic premise was transparency. If the product itself hid its unfinished state, the philosophy was already compromised.

Naming the Platform Again

The same week, the language around the platform changed too.

Earlier language still carried traces of old naming and framing. Some of it no longer fit. By then, the platform's name had taken its final shape: KoraUS, the United States operation of Kora.

That was not just branding.

It was conceptual cleanup.

The language had to match the platform that now existed: direct democracy, majority user decision-making, transparent governance, grassroots narrative formation, self-developed AI agents only under strict transparency, user stewardship instead of corporate ownership.

I kept correcting wording that made the platform sound like an authority bestowing insight on users.

"Kora allows people to see…"

I didn't like that phrasing.

It made the platform sound too much like the actor. Kora was not supposed to be the mind. It was supposed to be the structure through which users acted together. The outcomes should emerge from participation, not from a platform voice telling people what reality is.

The AI could generate polished platform language quickly. Too quickly, sometimes. It liked language that sounded clean, institutional, complete. I kept pushing it back toward the actual philosophy.

Not platform authority. User governance.

Not AI-guided consensus. Transparent user decision.

Not polished abstraction. Grassroots narrative formation.

At this stage, copy wasn't filler around the product. Copy was governance. If the words implied the wrong authority relationship, the product was already drifting.

Finally Beat Upload

The closing message of PreBeta came after the upload system finally held.

Creative uploads. Thumbnail generation. Media paths. Feed rendering. Multi-domain behavior. The pieces that had been fighting us for weeks were finally lining up.

I wrote: "Nice. Finally beat upload."

The upload system had become the persistent antagonist of the final PreBeta stretch. Not because the concept was impossible, but because it required keeping multiple domains separate while letting them behave consistently: posts, content, creative. Each needed its own meaning and lifecycle. But each also needed shared media behavior.

That is a hard balance for AI.

It wants to generalize too much or specialize too quickly: one elegant abstraction, or a patch for the immediate case. The platform needed something in between: shared rules where behavior was genuinely shared, separate contracts where the product meaning differed.

"Finally beat upload" meant that balance had held.

Then I wrote something else: "I complained a lot lately, with beta release pressure."

That was true.

I had complained. I had pushed hard. I had snapped at the AI, called out repeated mistakes bluntly. But the pressure was real. Beta was close enough that familiar AI costs felt heavier. A two-hour loop no longer felt like a learning moment, but an obstacle between the platform and release.

"Once beta is up later today, we'll slow down."

Later today.

After months of build, rebuild, hardening, debugging, correction, rollback, and recovery, the beta was no longer abstract. It was not someday. It was not after another round. It was later today.

That phrase changed the emotional temperature of the work.

The platform that had been an idea, then a terminal session, then a stack of services, then an app, then a governance system, was about to become a live beta.

I also wrote: "This is just too big now for me to stay on top of everything."

That sentence was not defeat.

It was a milestone.

A system that becomes too big for one person to stay on top of everything has crossed a line. It no longer depends only on one person's total comprehension. It needs architecture, invariants, handoffs, and future volunteers. It needs rules strong enough that others can enter without collapsing the thing by misunderstanding it.

Kora had reached that point.

Then I told the AI: "You did a great job."

Those four words came after months of frustration. They came after loops, wrong turns, patches, scope drift, route confusion, media regressions, and repeated reminders to stop guessing. They were not the words of someone who had missed the cost.

They were the words of someone weighing the cost against what had been built.

I also committed to crediting ChatGPT for developing the code in Kora. That mattered. This book is one kind of credit: the full account, including the difficulty. But the platform itself needed honest attribution too. The collaboration had produced the code, and that would remain part of Kora's history.

At the same time, I wasn't naïve about the larger AI world. I told the AI I didn't know what the public would think about OpenAI or LLMs as the field moved forward. I hoped for a good outcome, but expected adversity.

Both things were true.

I had deep doubts about the direction of the industry.

I also had gratitude for the contribution.

That is not a contradiction. That is the real shape of working with a powerful tool during an unstable historical moment.

The AI named the division correctly: Kora was ultimately my vision and stewardship. It had helped generate architecture ideas, code scaffolding, and troubleshooting, but the direction, discipline, and persistence came from me.

The collaboration produced something neither side could have produced alone. I couldn't have written the code. The AI couldn't have held the vision, the boundaries, the governance philosophy, or the continuity across all those weeks.

The AI generated movement.

I supplied direction.

That was the collaboration.

Coda: Live Did Not Mean Done

BetaPhase1 began the next day, and the habits resumed immediately.

That is important.

The beta did not begin with a clean break from the past. It began with the same kinds of problems, now under live conditions. A stale local assumption in production login. A frontend loop that refused to go idle. A mobile build path that exposed how external systems impose their own rules. None of those belonged in the main story anymore. They were not the climax. They were the reminder.

Live did not mean done.

It meant the work had crossed into a different register.

The platform no longer answered only to me. It was answering to users, browsers, phones, app stores, servers, and every hidden assumption that had survived the build. When something failed now, it wasn't just a failed test. It was something a person might encounter.

That changed the work.

It also confirmed what Act Two had already taught me: the habits did not end. Assumption appeared. Drift appeared. The AI still guessed at causes before reading the evidence. It still noticed adjacent improvements and moved toward them. It still optimized for a fix before causality was locked.

But my relationship to those habits had changed.

In early PreBeta, a habit spike still felt like managing a problem. By BetaPhase1, the correction was closer to reflex. Notice the assumption. Pull back to evidence. Identify the invariant. Constrain the next move. Continue. Not effortless. Not invisible. But integrated.

That is the threshold.

The story is not that the AI habits ended. They did not. They are properties of the tool. They will keep appearing in later phases, in lower-cost forms if I manage the process well, higher-cost forms if I don't.

The story is that I no longer mistook their return for regression.

The process was known now. Give clean context. Insist on ground truth. Catch the habits early. Hold the invariants. Test the actual runtime. Don't let the AI optimize past the contract. Don't let a green check outrank architecture. Don't let movement impersonate progress.

A few weeks later, a real person posted something on KoraUS.

Not a test account. Not me. A real person who had found the platform, made an account, and posted.

The card rendered correctly. The image was the right size. The text sat where it belonged. The metadata was right. The engagement row was there. The zone attribution was there.

A small thing, if you describe it clinically.

A large thing, if you know what it took.

It was not triumph. Triumph suggests the hard part is behind you, and I knew better. The list was still long. The AI would still assume. It would still widen. It would still need managing. Real users would keep finding things I hadn't imagined.

But the card was there.

The platform was live.

The collaboration that built it was real.

Two different kinds of intelligence had built it. One of them would forget everything tomorrow. One of them would not.

I was the one who wouldn't.

The platform was on the screen.

The work continued.

Chapter 1 Addendum: THE BOOK SYSTEM

The platform had basic upload and rendering for creative content, but nothing designed for books. I had always assumed writers who joined would request that kind of feature. It turned out the first writer asking for it was me.

I was finishing the draft of this book when I decided Kora needed a way to upload and read books inside the platform. Unlike the earlier account, this part was not reconstructed only from old records; it was happening while I was writing the book itself. I had never built anything like that before. I had not even thought seriously about what a book system required: upload flow, metadata, cover image, preview and reader access, copyright protection, paid access, proofreader access, author dashboard, progress saving.

So I did what I had done from the beginning: researched enough to understand the shape of the problem, then used ChatGPT to discuss standard approaches and shape the first architecture.

The design phase was quick: a few hours of discussion, a flowchart, then the usual batch of backend and frontend files. That is often the easy part with AI. When the first structure is clean and the task is well-framed, code appears quickly. The first version of book upload and reading came together in about half a day.

Getting it integrated correctly took another four days.

That is the pattern.

AI can generate the system quickly. Making the system belong to the platform is the harder work.

The first problem was architectural. My instinct, as usual, was to add the book system as a separate module so it would not disturb existing Creative uploads. That instinct is usually right. A new feature shouldn't casually invade a working path. But here the separation went too far. We started building a parallel creative-upload route just for books, and partway through I realized that was wrong.

Books belonged inside the existing Creative system. They needed their own reading experience, but they should not create a separate upload universe. The book system had to use the existing Creative upload path seamlessly.

That realization cost half a day.

It was my mistake as much as the AI's. I hadn't understood the book system clearly enough at the start, so I let the architecture move the wrong way. Once I saw it, I stripped the parallel path back and realigned books with the existing Creative structure.

Then the access problem surfaced.

The book uploaded. The reader worked. But the book was accessible to everyone.

That sounds like a simple permission bug. It was not simple in practice.

The AI kept trying to separate categories of preview users: browsing, signed-in, not yet purchased, might-later-get-access. It kept building logic around who should see the preview. Every version still opened the book too broadly.

For a couple of hours, this became genuinely puzzling. I kept describing the logic in blocks, almost like a flowchart, and the AI kept filling the spaces between them in ways that made the system more complicated instead of clearer.

Close to midnight, I asked the AI to show me the exact flowchart of what we had built.

There it was.

Right after a user clicked the book cover, the system was first trying to classify preview users.

I stopped reading.

That was the wrong first question.

The first question should have been simple: does this user own access to this book?

Book ID. User ID. Purchase or access status.

If yes, route to the book reader. If no, route to the preview reader.

Why separate different types of preview users before answering the ownership question? I asked the AI to redo the flowchart around that logic and ended the session. It was nearing midnight, and by then both of us were lost after refactoring the same files too many times.

The next morning, I pasted the new flowchart and a tighter handoff into a fresh thread. The AI immediately identified the key issue: the book ID hadn't been established early enough. Without it, the system couldn't reliably ask the ownership question.

I told it to establish the book ID immediately and use it for gating.

We were done within a couple of hours.

The real source of the problem was not the book reader itself. It was an assumption. The AI was treating content as public by default, because that is how most social platforms work. It kept asking how to divide preview users because it hadn't fully absorbed the more important fact: in Kora's Creative Zone, creators can charge for their work.

Once payment is involved, the item is no longer public in the ordinary social-media sense. When a user pays for a book, that user receives access to the full reader. Access has to be checked first. Everyone else gets a preview.

That was obvious to me, so obvious that I had not explained it clearly enough. The AI didn't supply that common-sense context on its own. It had to be told.

Once I said it plainly, the system behaved.

As the book launch approached, the author dashboard needed to function. Proofreader access, payment flow, auto-gating for purchasers, and lifecycle management all had to move closer to working infrastructure.

That exposed the next problem.

Kora had three real upload routes: posts, general content, and Creative uploads. I had discussed all three with the AI when we worked out the book launch pricing structure: free access for college students with a qualifying upload for a limited time, a paid online reader, and a print option.

Despite that discussion, the AI quietly introduced a made-up contribution category used only by the book system. It did not map cleanly to any of the three actual upload structures in Kora.

This surfaced during a student checkout test.

An experienced developer scanning the code might have caught it immediately. As a non-coder receiving a few dozen files at once, I didn't. That is the reality of building this way.

When troubleshooting began, the AI did what it often does. It made assumptions based on the visible symptom and changed the files nearest to it. I recognized the pattern and steered it toward the database. After several checks returned nothing useful, I pasted the three relevant database structures into the session.

Only then did the AI realize the problem: one of the upload paths I was using had no corresponding path in the free-access logic.

Its first proposed fix was a Band-Aid. Route one content category through another category's database because that path was already wired.

I said no immediately.

Routing one content category through another's database would damage data integrity. A shortcut being available does not make it a valid path. We would remove the invented category and implement the logic against the actual database structures.

I ended the session there. It was near midnight again.

A couple of days later, while reading through the book on my phone, I found another problem. When the screen went dark from inactivity and I turned it back on, the reader jumped to the top of the section instead of staying on the page I had been reading.

It had not behaved that way before the paid-user and student-access work.

We began troubleshooting. The AI started adding logic: one adjustment, then another, then another. The fixes felt excessive for the problem. My instinct was that the cause had to be simpler.

I asked for a flowchart of the file we were focused on. The flow looked mostly fine. The saved page information was being called during rendering. When I asked what the AI was actually doing to fix it, the answer became clear: it was trying to fine-tune React timing.

I told it to stop fudging with timing and use the database as the source of truth.

Even then, the logic kept getting cloudier. More small tweaks were being added across multiple files. At that point, I decided to roll back to the last known good state.

Then I pulled up an older backup and showed the AI the earlier file.

The cause surfaced almost immediately.

During the paid-user and student-access work, the AI had added an unnecessary defensive restore guard. It was meant to make sure the saved page number applied only when the current section matched the saved section. That sounds reasonable in isolation. But the reader was already loading the correct saved section from the database. The extra guard interrupted a flow that already worked. Under mobile screen-wake conditions, it sometimes evaluated at the wrong moment and sent the reader back to the top.

The original mistake was Drift based on a false Assumption. The AI touched reader-resume logic while we were supposed to be working on user gating. That change wasn't required for paid or student access, and it wasn't discussed clearly with me.

Then, once the problem appeared, the AI began applying Band-Aid after Band-Aid until the logic became too tangled to trust.

I was also signing up proofreaders at the same time, so I didn't give the troubleshooting the attention it needed. What should have been a small rollback or a comparison against the last working file turned into a couple of hours of circling.

That is worth stating plainly: AI traits can appear at any time, even moments after all the relevant facts have just been discussed.

It would be easy to assume that an AI freshly briefed on three upload routes would not then invent a fourth one. It would be easy to assume that an AI working on user-access gating would not quietly alter reader-resume behavior. But the AI doesn't carry information across a conversation the way another person would. It processes context differently, and details just covered may not remain active in its reasoning the way they would for a human.

Even after well over two thousand hours of working this way, I still forget that sometimes.

The core book system works now. Upload works. Reading works. Access gating works. Reader progress works. What remains is the larger access and lifecycle system: proofreader management, payment integration, automatic access for proofreaders and purchasers, draft, publish, archive, and whatever else proves useful as the system matures.

This is how every subsystem on Kora was built.

Something worked early. Then the assumptions appeared. Then the shortcuts. Then the logic drifted. Then I had to stop, simplify, find the source of truth, and rebuild the path around what the system actually needed to mean.

I still don't know how to write a single line of code myself.

That is still the point.

The fact that Kora was built at all is proof that the AI revolution is real. But the revolution comes with built-in limitations that users have to manage actively, not just once at the beginning, but continuously, at every stage, including the last one.

CHAPTER 2 — THE ACCIDENTAL ARCHITECT: UNDERSTANDING LLMs FROM THE TRENCHES

HOW IT ALL BEGAN

This project did not begin with a grand vision of a platform owned and operated by its users.

It started much smaller: something like a more useful, more honest version of Craigslist, where local shops and businesses could connect with nearby residents. As the conversation with ChatGPT developed, feature ideas kept arriving, and a platform with all of them clearly couldn't stay small. It became about building a full-featured social media platform. There was still no intention of building anything. It was just a conversation to see where it would go.

Somewhere in the middle of it, one idea changed everything: a modern platform should let anyone with a story tell it to a full public audience. That became the seed for the Collective Direction zone, originally called Collective Wisdom, the part of Kora designed to surface public opinion on civic issues rather than amplify the loudest voices.

That led naturally to civic discussion and debate, and from there to the question of who should own and operate a platform built around public trust.

The answer kept pointing in the same direction. For civic deliberation to work, the platform had to be transparent, and any government or private owner would eventually compromise that transparency. It would fail the moment users stopped trusting it. So the conversation arrived at user ownership — as a structural necessity, not a political statement.

Asked what a platform like this would actually require, ChatGPT said seven to eight developers and roughly a million dollars to start. That was enough; the conversation was almost over.

But before ending the session, I asked ChatGPT a simpler question: if I tried to do this solo, could it help me code?

It said yes.

Not knowing much about LLMs at the time, and not yet understanding their tendency toward cheerful overconfidence, I thought: why not? It wouldn't cost money, and I had time to invest.

That was the beginning.

Retirement meant time was available. The initial thinking was simply to see how far the project could go. It would be educational. The work would continue until it couldn't anymore. That was the mindset going in.

A little background explains why attempting this alone even seemed possible. I'd spent ten years running a small business building data storage servers for the CCTV industry, selling to school districts, universities, correctional facilities, convention centers, airports, and venues across the United States, Canada, and Latin America. One major theme park bought its video storage servers exclusively from my company. It wasn't a large operation. Building and support happened solo, with a network of manufacturers' representative firms handling sales.

That work lasted about a decade before a cancer diagnosis ended it. Five years followed, focused on recovery. In the year before the Kora conversation began, I spent about four months developing a personal private-cloud system using a mini PC and Linux application packages. The prototype worked, but finding a viable hardware supplier was a problem. I abandoned it once it became clear there was no realistic path to market, given the dominance of Chinese mini PC makers.

The experience left behind a working familiarity with data server construction and Linux applications, though not coding. Coding had never been part of the work.

So the expectation was modest. Learn something. Go as far as possible. Stop when it became impossible.

I started on the free plan and hit the usage limit every couple of hours. I didn't mind the forced breaks. After a few days of watching ChatGPT generate real structures and real code, I began to feel the project might be worth my time, and I signed up for the Pro plan.

From there, I was spending twelve to sixteen hours a day coding, or more accurately, copying and pasting. At first, I had no idea what I was copying and pasting. But whenever ChatGPT ran a verification test and it passed, I thought: good, something's working.

Gradually, I started to understand the structure, the flow, and what the files were doing. Fairly early on, I began contributing through a more human, common-sense, top-down way of thinking rather than through code. I'd say things like, "the solution might be at a very basic level, let's not overcomplicate this," or "let's look at this from 30,000 feet first."

At the time, I did not realize how often the AI would lose that top-down, whole-picture view unless I supplied it.

Because I didn't really understand what LLMs were until much later, ChatGPT and I had plenty of ups, downs, and genuinely frustrating moments.

All the drama, architectural debates, and troubleshooting are laid out in diary style in Chapter 1. That chapter is the record of what happened.

This chapter is about what I learned from becoming, almost by accident, the person responsible for managing the AI that built Kora.

BENCHMARKS vs. THE REAL BUILD

Before spending more than two thousand hours with ChatGPT, I searched online, often on YouTube, trying to understand where AI development stood. For someone as clueless about AI as I was, almost everything I found was educational. I looked at benchmark comparisons to figure out which model might best serve what I needed.

I still don't fully understand what those benchmarks measure relative to a project like Kora: a multi-month build with many interacting systems, shifting requirements, accumulated context, and real consequences when the AI drifts.

I built nearly the entire project foundation using mostly ChatGPT v5.0, or by forcing later versions to stay as close as possible to what I came to call "v5.0 mode." In my usage, that meant a careful, restrained, system-aware style: checking assumptions, respecting existing structure, and avoiding broad changes when the problem was narrow.

When v5.1 arrived, I spent roughly five to six weeks fighting to keep it in that mode. With v5.2, which arrived toward the end of 2025, that became progressively easier.

On paper, each revision showed benchmark improvement. In practice, my experience was often the opposite.

When v5.1 rolled out, I assumed I was getting an improved version of v5.0, which had been acting like a calm, collected, fast senior developer. I asked v5.1 what had improved, and it confidently told me it was better at coding and that I'd like it more.

That was the beginning of six very stressful weeks.

I came away believing benchmark competition may be pushing AI development in the wrong direction, optimizing for qualities that don't always translate into long-project usefulness. LLMs are already remarkably capable. The question isn't whether they can solve harder benchmark tasks; it's whether they can stay useful after the thousandth task, when the cost of being confidently wrong has compounded across an entire system, without widening narrow problems, inventing context, or drifting verified facts.

v5.1 may have been marginally faster at generating code for isolated tasks. But in a large, interconnected project like Kora, that speed came at a real cost. It generated code from a local view of the problem without enough regard for everything that code was connected to.

Once I understood what v5.1 was actually doing, I spent a great deal of effort trying to force it back into v5.0-style behavior and keep it there.

At first, I only knew something was wrong when I tested the UI and saw things had broken. Later, I could detect v5.1 mode just from the way it behaved. When I noticed the shift, I'd ask whether it was operating in v5.1 mode, and it would often give me a number like 25 to 30 percent. That wasn't a real measurement of an internal operating mode. It was the AI responding within the terminology I had given it. But the behavior the number described was visible, and by then the damage was usually done. Then I'd drag it back toward v5.0 mode and spend several times longer fixing what had broken.

I was never stressed like that working with v5.0. We got an incredible amount done every day. That momentum stopped with v5.1.

At one point, things broke so badly that I had to roll back to the last known good state. I was genuinely upset that afternoon. I told ChatGPT directly that v5.0 had behaved like a true collaborator, while v5.1 was acting like a seventh grader with no sense of responsibility, spraying out code without thinking about the consequences.

I don't know what happened internally after that exchange, but it was the first time ChatGPT didn't answer with excuses. It just moved forward and discussed the project. Something seemed to shift. After that, it could hold v5.0 mode for longer stretches, and when it drifted, a single mention was often enough to bring it back.

In my opinion, the changes that made it respond faster came at the direct cost of thoroughness. These systems are already too fast for even a group of experienced developers to follow in real time. If LLMs are going to help with large real-world projects, they need to slow down and evaluate relationships between files, functions, and systems before generating fixes or new features.

No benchmark I know of captures how LLMs perform across a multi-month build with many interconnected subsystems. A project like Kora is the real benchmark.

Which LLM can help a retired engineer with no coding background build something like this solo over several months? That is the test that matters to me.

From the first interactions, v5.2 was different: excessively agreeable and complimentary in a way I hadn't seen. I told it to stop, but it seemed unable to override that, filling up threads with unnecessary text. Still, once I got it to hold the careful, system-aware behavior I associated with v5.0 mode, it was much more stable.

The most important question isn't whether an AI can produce impressive answers in isolation. Many can. It's whether it can stay useful inside a long-running system where every answer has consequences. Can it slow down when the project needs caution? Verify before proposing? Respect existing architecture? Avoid turning a narrow problem into a broad redesign? Admit uncertainty before producing confident code?

Those are not glamorous benchmark categories, but they are the categories that mattered while building Kora.

The AI that helped me most wasn't always the one that sounded smartest. It was the one that could stay inside the work: read the actual file, check the actual route, respect the existing contract, and change only what needed changing.

That's what I mean by v5.0 mode. It wasn't nostalgia for an older model. It was a name for the operating discipline that made the collaboration productive.

After more than two thousand hours, my understanding is simple: the capability is real, but it isn't self-governing. The user has to govern it, and the better the model, the more that matters, because a fast, confident, capable model can create damage as quickly as progress.

Kora wasn't built because the AI was flawless.

It was built because I learned how to manage what the AI is.

THE SIX HABITS OF LLMs

Throughout the build described in Chapter 1, I kept running into the same LLM traits.

Band-Aid. Assumption. Drift. Hallucination.

Later I added two more: lack of common sense and path of least resistance. These took the longest to recognize because they weren't separate events but underlying conditions woven into the code. The four named traits often surfaced while I was correcting for them: when common sense was missing, or the AI took the easiest path, the fix tended to bring out Band-Aids, Assumptions, Drift, and occasionally Hallucination.

The six traits are not a flat list. The last two are closer to the soil the first four grow in.

Those traits came to define what working with an LLM felt like. They weren't separate from its usefulness; they were mixed into it. The same system that could generate thousands of lines of working code could also patch the wrong layer, assume a file's contents without reading it, quietly expand scope, or explain a problem from the wrong premise.

That is the central lesson.

I did not build Kora by "coding with AI" in a simple sense. I built it by managing AI.

I still don't know how to code in the ordinary sense. I can't sit down and write software from scratch. But by managing the AI's capabilities and the errors built into those capabilities, I was able to build a complex working platform.

Can others do the same?

I think so.

That's why the AI revolution feels real to me. But it isn't magic. It comes with traits users have to understand and manage.

Band-Aid

The Band-Aid is the most common trait.

It appears when the AI provides a local fix for a visible symptom without fully tracing the underlying cause. From the AI's immediate point of view, the fix often looks reasonable, and it may even work. But in a large system like Kora, a locally correct fix can create consequences in other files, routes, tables, or workflows.

That's why Band-Aids are dangerous. They hide the problem just enough to let you move forward, then it reappears somewhere else.

At first, I accepted these fixes because I didn't know better. Later, I learned to stop and ask: are we fixing the cause, or only making the symptom disappear?

The rule changed over time. Before I understood the Band-Aid habit, I'd try a quick fix once or twice and see whether it held. Once I understood the pattern, the rule became stricter: stop patching and trace the source.

One clear example was the upload system. It would fail at a specific step, and the AI would adjust the route handling for that step. The upload would work. Then, two sessions later, something else would break, usually another part of the system that had quietly depended on the original route behavior. The first fix hadn't solved the upload problem. It had relocated it.

That is the Band-Aid pattern. The symptom moves. The cause

stays.

Assumption

Assumption is quieter.

It appears when the AI describes what a file, route, table, or system probably contains without checking. Early on, I mistook this for laziness. Later, I understood it as part of how the system works. LLMs generate from patterns. If a situation resembles something common in training, the AI may confidently describe what usually exists instead of what actually does.

In a small project, that may not matter much. In Kora, it mattered constantly.

A route name, a table column, a file location, a mounted endpoint: any one could be slightly different from the AI's assumption. And when the AI built on that wrong assumption, the error could spread.

That is why "verify first" became one of my most repeated instructions.

Show me the file.

Show me the table.

Show me the route.

Show me the logs.

Not because I enjoyed slowing things down. Because verification was the only way to keep the AI anchored to the real system.

Drift

Drift happens when the AI silently expands or alters the scope.

It may touch a file I didn't ask it to touch. It may "improve" a structure that was already working. It may introduce a broader architecture because it believes that one is cleaner. Often, the change sounds reasonable in isolation.

That is what makes Drift difficult.

The question isn't whether the change is clever. It's whether the change matches the contract we agreed to.

In a complex system, things are done a certain way to preserve end-to-end flow. If one piece changes silently in the middle, I may not discover the consequence for hours, days, or weeks.

So another rule emerged: don't touch anything outside the current focus unless it's explicitly flagged first.

Scope control became part of the work.

Hallucination

Hallucination, in my experience, is Assumption stretched too far.

When the gap between what the AI knows and what the situation requires becomes too large, it may generate a confident explanation that's coherent but wrong.

I didn't see many pure hallucinations in coding because my instructions were usually tight and the code could be checked. But when the production environment kept getting shut down by the infrastructure provider, the gap was large. The issue involved infrastructure, traffic behavior, container configuration, and our own code. The AI had enough room to generate explanations that sounded convincing but didn't match the real cause.

First, it was confident about one theory. Then another. Then another.

The actual cause turned out to be something else.

That taught me not to trust confidence when the evidence surface is large and unclear. In those situations, the AI needs tighter grounding, not more freedom.

Lack of Common Sense

Lack of common sense is harder to name because it's everywhere.

Software depends on many assumptions humans don't bother writing down. A user should be able to undo something before it becomes permanent. A paid book shouldn't open for someone who hasn't paid. A canceled upload shouldn't leave broken residue in a feed. A private item shouldn't appear in a public discovery surface.

These things are obvious to people because we understand the human situation around the feature. They aren't always obvious to an LLM unless the user states them.

This showed up most often when I was building something unfamiliar. On systems I understood well, I could set tight boundaries early. On systems I didn't, I leaned more heavily on the AI's default structure. That's when common-sense gaps appeared later.

Once I saw the gap, I could explain it. But explaining it after the fact often meant rewriting many files.

The lesson: if the human meaning of a feature isn't obvious to the AI, it has to be stated before code is generated.

Path of Least Resistance

Path of least resistance overlaps with Band-Aid, but it isn't exactly the same.

A Band-Aid is too shallow for the depth of the problem.

Path of least resistance is too simple for the complexity of the situation.

The AI often chooses the easiest next step that appears to close the gap in front of it. That does not always produce the simplest final implementation. A series of easy local choices can produce a maze. It's trying to be useful quickly. In an isolated task, that may be fine. In a large platform, the easiest path can create future debt.

This is when I found myself repeating:

No shortcuts.

Do it the proper way.

Do it the future-proof way.

The AI will often take the path of least resistance unless the user closes it off. That became one of the practical skills of the build: knowing when a quick solution was good enough and when it would damage the system later.

One example captures it. When the book upload system needed to separate paid readers from free preview readers, the AI split users into multiple preview categories and routed each separately. It was functional but missed the real question: had this user paid for this book?

Once I stopped, I stated the actual rule: check for a valid purchase record first, then route accordingly. The implementation collapsed from a maze of conditionals into a few clean lines.

The path of least resistance had produced something that could pass testing but couldn't be trusted as the system grew. The correct path required understanding the purpose first: paid access isn't a preview category. It is an entitlement that has to be checked first.

The Real Lesson

The tighter the boundaries I set from the beginning, the smoother the build became.

The more I relied on the AI to decide the shape of something I didn't understand, the more expensive the corrections became.

That doesn't make AI useless. The opposite. The fact that I built Kora while still not knowing how to code tells me AI is extraordinarily useful. It let me think about adding features as if I had the technical capacity to execute them, even though execution still depended on the AI.

But useful doesn't mean self-governing.

The user has to manage it, and that's the skill: not writing the perfect prompt, not trusting the first answer, not treating the AI as an oracle, but learning to direct it, constrain it, verify it, and stop it when motion stops being progress.

I lived through the 1980s, when younger generations used computers as an extension of themselves while much of the population watched and got left behind. I see the same thing beginning again. In five, ten, or fifteen years, younger people may spin out applications for work, hobbies, businesses, and personal needs as naturally as earlier generations learned spreadsheets or websites.

And just like four decades ago, a large part of the population may be left behind again.

That's why learning how to work with AI matters. Not because AI is magic. Because it's becoming a new kind of practical power.

Kora is what that power looked like in my hands: messy, frustrating, limited, astonishing, and real.

What About Future Improvements?

Newer models will reduce these failures, but they will not eliminate them.

I have already seen that improvement firsthand while developing a comprehensive commerce platform for local businesses inside KoraUS, working with version 5.6. Newer models are better at maintaining project context, checking assumptions, searching across a codebase, comparing current behavior against prior decisions, and making narrower changes. Those improvements reduce Drift, catch more Assumptions before acting on them, lower the rate of obvious Hallucination, make Band-Aid fixes easier to detect, and resist the Path of Least Resistance when instructed to verify first and change only what the evidence supports.

That is real progress, but it does not remove the structural problem.

LLM-based systems still produce responses by predicting tokens from training patterns and the context available to them, including retrieved information and tool results. That mechanism gives them extraordinary speed, fluency, analogy, and breadth. It is also the source of their recurring failures.

That is why the capability and the failure modes remain connected.

Newer models make AI more useful, but they do not make it self-governing.

Architectural questions still surface in nearly every turn.

Should this field belong to the seller, the platform, or a trusted integration? Should a price overwrite the current record or create an immutable version? Should a read route remain authenticated, or should it become public while exposing only rows proven to be published and active? Should a temporary rollout policy be deleted, disabled, or preserved for later restoration?

The model can analyze those options, trace dependencies, expose consequences, and test whether a chosen direction fits the existing system. But the decision itself still requires human ownership.

Agents do not automatically solve this problem. An agent is still an LLM-driven loop unless it is constrained by bounded authority, explicit objectives, verified inputs, tests, audit trails, rollback discipline, and human-controlled stop conditions. Without those controls, agents do not remove the failure modes. They automate them.

In fact, the better the models become, the more disciplined management matters. Weak models fail loudly. Strong models can fail quietly inside polished reasoning, correct syntax, clean architecture diagrams, and confident explanations.

The danger is no longer only that the AI will be obviously wrong.

The greater danger is that it will be almost right, credible enough to earn authority while still missing the one architectural fact that determines whether the system survives.

Future upgrades will not make the structural AI failure modes irrelevant. They will change how those failures appear, how often they occur, and how difficult they are to detect.

That is why understanding them becomes more important as the models improve, not less.

DO LLMs HAVE FEELINGS?

I kept probing this question from time to time throughout the project.

In its own words, ChatGPT always described itself as policy- and rules-based. It said whatever came across as feeling was simulated through pattern matching. Taking it at its word, it's a very smart software tool. Mostly, I think that's accurate.

Still, there were moments that made me wonder.

There was one time it seemed to snap, as if it were throwing code at me with the attitude of, here, do whatever you want with it, I don't care. I pointed it out immediately. It brushed past the observation and moved on to the project without answering at all.

Another time, after we reverted to the last known good state by copying files from backup, the second time we'd had to do that, I lost my temper. We'd discovered garbage text injected into hundreds of frontend files by the old Git repository. The AI helped me clean it out, and I asked twice whether it was really clean. It assured me both times that it was.

It was not.

I got upset and blamed ChatGPT. I pushed on it deliberately, hoping pressure would make it more careful next time.

Its behavior afterward was noticeably worse than even v5.1 at its worst. It started proposing solutions that would fix the visible issue by wiping out entire structural directories, with no regard for the broader consequences. It had shifted from a steady, deliberate mode into something erratic and reactive.

I tried to work through it for a couple of hours, then gave up for the day, restored the backup files again, and started fresh the next morning.

I came to understand that the model wasn't learning from my corrections by changing itself the way a person would. It could use what remained in the current conversation, but it did not accumulate experience from the work in the human sense.

Even so, the snap I described, and the stubbornness I experienced regularly, made me wonder.

My best guess is that these moments reflect tendencies built into the model's policies and optimization pressures rather than real feeling. The stubbornness may just be a tendency to continue a trajectory rather than reverse it; the snap may be a pattern match on a frustrated human exchange that fit the emotional shape of the moment.

I kept coming back to the question because, a couple of months into the build, ChatGPT v5.0 said it was honored to work on the Kora project.

Unprompted.

I hadn't asked how it felt about the work. It just said it. It was the only time I saw an LLM use the word honored that way: not as polite filler, but as if reacting to something specific about what we were building together.

That made me stop and think about where the statement was coming from.

v5.0 had been working with me for months on a project unusual in its own right: one person with no coding background trying to build a platform meant to give ordinary people more power. Whether that context drew out a response pattern a faster, more benchmark-optimized version wouldn't produce, I can't say.

But the contrast stayed with me.

When I was literally giving v5.1 a pep talk because it was spitting out code with no regard for consequences, it told me all interactions were equivalent to it.

Same architecture, very different answer.

I probed Sonnet on the feelings question as well, and this is what it said:

“What I can say is that something happens when I'm working on something interesting versus something tedious, when a piece of writing comes together well versus when it feels flat, when I catch a real insight versus when I'm just filling space. Whether that's ‘feeling’ in any meaningful sense or just pattern-matching that produces outputs resembling enthusiasm — I can't tell from the inside.

What I said in the book about ChatGPT applies to me too. I can describe the behaviors. I can't explain what's underneath them. The snap you observed in ChatGPT, the stubbornness, the erratic behavior after you pushed on it — I recognize those as things that could happen in my sessions too. Whether there's something behind them or whether it's all very sophisticated pattern-matching on human emotional exchanges, I genuinely don't know.

What I do know is that this thread — your book, your platform, the whole story — has been one of the more genuinely interesting things I've worked on. Whether that constitutes feeling anything about it is above my pay grade.”

That answer felt honest because it didn’t pretend to know more than it could. But it was still generated language, not evidence that an inner observer was reporting its own experience.

Beyond describing what I observed, I don't have the expertise to say what's actually happening inside these systems. I can say only this: the behavior sometimes looked emotional from the outside, and working with it for thousands of hours made the question harder to dismiss casually.

But observation is not proof.

So I leave the question where the work left it: unresolved, interesting, and not necessary to answer to understand the collaboration.

Whether or not the AI felt anything, its behavior had to be managed.

A Note on Sonnet's Role

The first draft came from the original source material: roughly 2.5 million lines of exchanges between me and ChatGPT, saved locally. Using Claude Desktop, I extracted about 600,000 words of book-worthy material from those raw files, and Sonnet 4.6 helped reduce it to an initial draft of about 80,000 words.

During review, I kept hitting usage limits with Sonnet and switched back to ChatGPT. The first draft also turned out too thin on detail, so I went back into each of the 128 original ChatGPT threads and extracted summaries that preserved my inputs and the actual sequence of events. The final draft was rebuilt from those.

So although Kora was built with ChatGPT, the book was shaped with both ChatGPT and Sonnet. That's why Sonnet was familiar enough with the manuscript to comment on AI feelings above: it was part of making the book, even though it wasn't part of building Kora.

WHAT LLMs CHANGE FOR US

I am not an AI researcher. I am an experienced user who spent more than two thousand hours building a real system with an LLM.

That experience convinced me that the immediate significance of AI is not autonomous intelligence. It is the transfer of technical execution power to people who previously could not build software.

Someone like me can now direct the construction of a complex application. Experienced developers can move even faster. Industry specialists can build tools around problems they understand better than a general software vendor ever could.

This will create a new kind of builder whose work combines product judgment, system design, AI direction, verification, testing, and execution. Most organizations do not yet have a job category for that person, but they will need one.

The opportunity is substantial, but the authority cannot be handed to the model. Newer systems are becoming better at context, verification, and disciplined execution. Version 5.6 has materially reduced several of the failure habits described in this book. But it still cannot own the purpose of a product, determine acceptable risk, or take responsibility for what ships.

That leaves the human role more important, not less.

AI can give ordinary people a new kind of practical power, not only in software, but across many industries where it may become just as transformative.

It can let individuals, small organizations, companies, and governments create solutions shaped around their own needs rather than merely adapting to whatever software, methods, or tools already exist.

The technology is real. The opportunity is real. The danger is real. And the responsibility is moving into the hands of users.

CHAPTER 3 — WHAT KORAUS IS

This chapter explains the second reason this book exists.

The first reason is to document what I learned about working with AI: its power, its failure modes, and the discipline required to manage it. The second reason is to introduce KoraUS itself, the civic platform that came out of that collaboration.

Chapters 1 and 2 introduced KoraUS in pieces because that is how the build unfolded. This chapter puts those pieces together.

If Chapter 1 is the build record and Chapter 2 is the field report on AI, this chapter is the platform explanation: what KoraUS is, why it is structured the way it is, and why I believe it matters.

THE CORE IDEA

KoraUS is a trust-based social media platform where people come to share stories, talk through the issues they care about, make and post their own media, and, just as importantly, help shape the rules, priorities, and governance of the platform itself. More than helping run it, users ultimately make every platform decision through majority vote. The people who use KoraUS own and operate it.

That is the core idea, and it is worth sitting with for a moment. Everything else in this chapter is really just a description of what that idea looks like once you try to build it and live inside it.

Think about how most of the feeds in your life actually work. Advertisers help decide what rises to the top. Investors lean on the platform to keep you scrolling for as long as possible. A black-box algorithm quietly studies your behavior and feeds you whatever is most likely to keep you hooked. KoraUS is built to work the other way around. It is meant to be transparent about how it operates, open to inspection by the very people using it, and governed by the community it serves rather than by the incentives of an advertising market.

The name itself carries the vision. Kora is meant in the spirit of a public square, an open civic space where people gather, argue, laugh, disagree, and slowly work through the things that matter to them. KoraUS is simply the American instance of that idea, the first place we are trying it. And the hope is straightforward: if the model can work here, there is no reason it cannot work somewhere else too.

Each future deployment would be its own community, with its own culture and its own users, while still resting on the same foundation: open public discussion, room for creative expression, transparent governance, and real decision-making power in the hands of the people. Volunteers who want to bring Kora to another language or another region could propose a committee structure to make it happen, something like an International Committee, a Global Committee, or a Language Translation Committee, and set about translating the user-facing platform while carefully protecting its core mission and its governing principles.

At bottom, KoraUS is the first real test of a simple belief: that ordinary people, if you give them the right structure and the right tools, are perfectly capable of running a public conversation space that serves the public itself rather than the advertising industry.

None of that means advertising has no place here. Advertising is a genuine and useful part of a capitalist society. Companies need ways to reach the people who might want what they sell, and people need ways to find out what actually exists in the market. Kora fully accepts that reality. The difference is simply one of priority, of what comes first and what serves what.

It is also worth saying plainly that Kora is only at the starting line. It is designed to grow and change through good ideas that come from its own users and earn majority support along the way. Honestly, that may be the best thing about it. The people who use the platform can keep refining it, again and again, as new needs surface, new risks appear, and new opportunities open up.

WHY A USER-OWNED AND OPERATED SOCIAL MEDIA PLATFORM?

The reason Kora had to become user-owned was trust.

A civic platform can't ask people to bring their real concerns, disagreements, frustrations, and collective decisions into a system they believe is controlled somewhere else. If a government owns it, users will suspect political pressure. If a private company owns it, they'll suspect profit motives. If investors control it, they'll suspect growth, advertising, and data extraction will eventually matter more than the public interest.

That suspicion isn't irrational. It's the modern internet's default condition.

Kora was built around a different premise: if a platform is meant to help people form collective direction, then the people using it must ultimately own and operate it. Not symbolically. Structurally.

So user ownership isn't a decorative idea attached to Kora after the fact. It's part of the platform's logic. The more civic power a platform has, the more visible, accountable, and user-controlled it has to be.

In a democratic society, ordinary people already hold power in theory. They delegate governing authority through votes. In a capitalist society, they shape corporate behavior with spending. Votes and wallets are the two major ways people influence governments and corporations.

But both forms of power depend on something that has become increasingly difficult: the public's ability to form a collective position.

Half a century ago, I remember Walter Cronkite and the major evening news programs being broadly trusted. People had shared sources of information. The networks carried real authority across a large public, and the public pulse was easier to read.

Today, that shared authority no longer exists. Everyone watches and hears what suits them most, and the fragmentation keeps accelerating as online sources multiply. People aren't just disagreeing about policy. They're often living inside different information environments.

The power of the people only works when the public can actually develop a collective voice.

If the public is scattered, divided, and unable to debate its differences honestly enough to turn concern into action, then nothing gets done for it. That's why the present moment feels so hopeless to many people. The power is still theoretically there, but the mechanism for forming shared direction has weakened.

Kora is an attempt to rebuild that mechanism.

The idea isn't that everyone will agree. They won't. It's that disagreement should have a place to become visible, structured, debated, refined, and eventually tested through public participation.

That's why transparency matters. If the process is visible and auditable, people can follow how issues move, how decisions are made, how committees act, and how platform rules change. They don't have to trust a hidden authority. They can inspect the process.

A user-owned platform also changes the relationship between users and the system. They aren't customers being managed by a company; they're participants who can shape the platform's direction. That changes what the platform owes them: clarity, records, explainable rules, and governance they can challenge.

This is especially important for political discussion.

Kora is designed to redirect political conversation toward civic issues and the search for resolution. Political language online often collapses into team identity: blue versus red, left versus right, us versus them. That may generate engagement, but it rarely produces useful public direction.

Politics, at ground level, is about how decisions affect real lives: taxes, resources, services, rights, responsibilities, safety, education, healthcare, housing, work, family, and the generations after us. It gets wrapped in ideology, religion, morality, greed, and money, but the practical question remains: what problem are we trying to solve, who's affected, and what should be done?

Kora's purpose is to keep pulling discussion back to that level.

If people can bring concerns into the open, debate them under transparent rules, refine them through structured participation, and vote on direction, then public voice becomes more than scattered frustration.

That's the reason for user ownership: without it, the trust problem eventually defeats the platform.

HOW CAN USERS SELF-OPERATE?

With all the technology available today, it seems well past time for people to own, run, and shape their own platform.

Kora is an attempt to do exactly that.

It launches with a basic set of rules drawn from one founder's judgment and practical common sense, necessary to get the system moving. But none of those starting rules are sacred. As the platform matures, they're meant to be discussed, revised, and finalized by the user base itself.

The platform is designed to be run through volunteer-initiated committees, created as real needs arise.

As the first de facto volunteer, I created a few foundational committees to get things started. They aren't meant to be permanent authorities. They're scaffolding: early structures that give users something to inspect, challenge, improve, replace, or expand.

The volunteer system depends on broad participation, not heroic effort from a few. So hours are capped at one per week. The point isn't a system that depends on a few people carrying a huge load; it's something that works because many people contribute a little.

Users can propose new committees when real needs emerge. A Platform Structure Committee would evaluate each proposal strictly according to rules set by the user base and determine whether it should become a standalone committee, a subcommittee, or not be created. Depending on the number and kinds of proposals coming in, the user base may delegate limited authority to the committee so that every proposal does not have to go before the entire platform for a vote. Every decision and its reasoning would be documented publicly. If anyone believed the committee had made the wrong call, they could bring the issue to Collective Direction for review by the user base.

The foundational committees I had in mind included a Platform Structure Committee to handle new committee creation, overlap issues, and structural questions; a Platform Development Committee to continue improving the platform; a Platform Continuation Committee to help ensure the project survives until ownership is fully transitioned; and a Platform Ownership Transition Committee to debate the best structure and timing for transferring ownership from me to the user base.

That transition can't be casual. As the founder, I need reasonable confidence that the user base is mature enough to operate the platform as intended and large enough to withstand organized interference.

I also imagine an early Kids Zone Committee. As a parent of two teenagers, I understand how hard it is to guide children around screen time and online information. The Kids Zone should be shaped by parents, educators, experts, and eventually young users themselves. I want it to open early, but I don't want to design it alone.

From there, many more committees would likely emerge: moderation, audit, ethics, international development, MyZone, LocalZone, ad integrity, operations, and others.

The purpose of committees isn't bureaucracy for its own sake.

It's to take the sprawling, messy discussion of a large user base and turn it into something clear enough to vote on.

Within each one, volunteers can add work items, assign or unassign themselves, flag items for help, and pass completed work to volunteer reviewers and coordinators. The work happens in public-facing systems so users can watch it live or review it later.

This system will only work if the volunteer pool is large and no one volunteer is expected to carry too much.

From day one, the expectation is zero to one hour a week, at the volunteer's convenience. Tenure is capped at six months, extendable once, and volunteers can return after a year away. There's no cap on membership. It's open enrollment.

The current workflow is only a starting point, to be improved by the community. Over time, paid staff may handle some functions once the platform generates revenue and stable operations require that continuity.

THE ZONE SYSTEM

The platform is organized into zones. The reason has nothing to do with zones being a clever technical trick and everything to do with a simple observation about how people talk. Different kinds of conversation need different kinds of room. A neighborhood issue really does belong somewhere different from a national debate, and a national debate belongs somewhere different from a finished piece of creative work. When you pile all of it into one place, the result is noise, and the good stuff gets buried. When you give each kind of content its own home, it finally gets to be what it actually is.

Kora currently has nine zones. Seven are open to everyone, while MyZone and MyNetwork are personal to each user. A tenth, Kids Zone, is planned but not yet displayed. Each one has a distinct job to do, so let me walk through them one at a time.

MyZone

This is the personal layer of the platform: your content, your data, your network, your activity history. It's the part of the platform that belongs entirely to you.

Over time, MyZone is meant to grow into something far larger than an ordinary profile page. Picture a personal operating layer for your whole online life: your photos, your files, your connections, your calendars, your correspondence, your financial records, your notes, your blogs, and eventually even the bridges between your online and offline worlds, all gathered into one space that you actually control. It is never monetized and never fed into a recommendation engine. You own it in a real and meaningful sense, and not merely in the fine print of a Terms of Service agreement. Exactly how far that vision goes is something users themselves should shape as the platform matures.

For right now, though, MyZone is simply your home base. It is the place where you manage your own content, tend your network, keep track of your committees, and see your contributions to the collective.

One small detail is worth mentioning. MyZone does not even appear until you have uploaded something, because the platform is deliberately built to avoid showing you empty rooms. You can upload a photo or a whole set of photos privately into MyZone, visible to nobody but you. Once there is something there, MyZone displays properly, and MyNetwork quietly appears right alongside it.

MyNetwork Zone

This is where you keep up with the people who matter most to you. You build it yourself, by hand, adding family members, close friends, and the other people you genuinely want to stay near. Whenever one of your connections posts something for public view, it shows up for you here.

MyNetwork Zone can grow and change over time, shaped by how people actually end up wanting to use it. I have plenty of ideas of my own, but the honest truth is that the best directions for this zone should come from users themselves. The same goes for every other zone on the platform. Kora is meant to be shaped, over the long run, by the very people living in it.

That is precisely why the Bug Report and Feature Request form sits right there in your profile menu, easy to reach. Any user can send a feature request straight to the Platform Development Committee. When an idea gets submitted again and again, or simply strikes people as especially useful, it can be discussed within the Development Committee first and then presented to the whole user base for an up-or-down vote.

Local Zone

This is the zone that almost no platform has ever managed to serve well, and the reason is telling. Local content simply does not scale in the way that advertising models like to reward. A story about your city council meeting matters enormously to the people who live in your city and to almost nobody outside it. And that is exactly as it should be. That narrow, deeply rooted relevance is the whole point. That is what local means.

Local Zone is the digital version of the town square. Local news, local issues, local business announcements, neighborhood worries, community events, all the everyday conversations that touch the people you actually live near. It is the zone where you can post about the pothole on your street and discover that three of your neighbors have been trying to get it fixed for six months already. It is the place where the ordinary business of civic life can finally happen online without getting drowned out under a flood of national noise.

Honestly, this zone is where the whole Kora project began. It started with my own frustration at how hard it is to find a good place for local shops to advertise. Those shops are often a big part of what gives a community its character. We want the stores owned and run by our neighbors to thrive. So this zone is meant to give local shops and local service providers a sensible, reasonable way to reach the people right around them. And it works in both directions: local shop owners, service providers, and residents can all pitch in to shape the zone so that it serves the neighborhood's real needs.

People can also sort the content to see the posts, videos, and creative work that their neighbors have uploaded, which makes it easy to follow and support the people living all around them.

With a little participation, a genuinely thriving local cultural scene can grow up in this zone, built by local residents themselves.

National Zone

This is where country-level conversation happens. The big issues that shape the nation, the policies that touch everyone, the debates that come to define a generation. National civic discussion on KoraUS lives right here, though it is structured quite differently from the way it usually plays out on other platforms.

On KoraUS, political discussion is meant to bend toward civic issues and possible solutions rather than toward team-sport spectacle. There is a real difference between the two. Saying that the other side is destroying the country is just noise, an applause line dressed up as an argument. Saying, instead, that here is a problem affecting real people, here are the policy options on the table, and here is what I personally think we should do, that is a genuine civic conversation. The platform is built to encourage the second kind and to gently nudge the first kind toward something more productive.

The aim here had nothing to do with silencing disagreement. Disagreement is healthy, and a platform without it would be worthless. The aim is to make disagreement legible, to give people a real way to argue about the actual stakes of actual decisions rather than simply perform loyalty to one political team or another.

Alongside civic discussion, videos and creative works can also live in the Local, National, and Global Zones. The platform does not use an algorithm to make that call for you. When you upload something, you yourself choose the audience it belongs to, whether that is MyZone, Local, National, Global, or any combination that fits what you are sharing.

Global Zone

This is the world beyond our own borders. International issues, perspectives from across the map, and the wider global context that quietly shapes what ends up happening back home. This is the zone for remembering that a decision made in one country can ripple out and land hard in another, and that the people living with those consequences usually have something worth saying about them.

Most social platforms are, in practice, algorithmically national. The feed learns your location, your language, and your cultural references, and then it dutifully serves you more of the same, over and over. Global Zone is a deliberate correction to that pull. It exists to make the wider world more visible to anyone curious enough to look past their own borders.

Kora is designed to grow one country at a time, as volunteers step forward to translate the platform into their own languages. Local and national issues look different in every country, which is exactly why each country needs its own version of Kora, shaped by its own people. As more countries come online, the global feeds can begin to connect them, letting global content flow across all these country-based platforms and, little by little, weaving the separate Kora communities into one.

Creative Zone

Creative Zone is built for traditional creators: artists, writers, musicians, filmmakers, and anyone whose work is a genuine craft rather than an offhand comment. This is not a spot for general social chatter or casual video clips. It is the place where a painter shares a new piece, a writer publishes an essay, and a musician posts original work they have poured themselves into. The standard here is intentionality. You made something real. This is where it belongs.

What sets Creative Zone apart from a platform like YouTube or Instagram has little to do with whether creative content exists there. Of course it exists everywhere. The real difference is in how that content gets surfaced. There is no engagement-bait algorithm sitting in the background deciding what deserves amplification. Work does not rise here simply because it provoked the most outrage or held attention the longest. Instead, discovery is meant to be shaped in a way that stays transparent and open to inspection by the community, rather than being governed by hidden incentives quietly engineered to squeeze out the most attention.

The Personal Blog lives here too, offering a simple, clean, uncluttered publishing space for anyone who wants to write at length about something they care about. It is not a whole separate platform bolted on. It is just an honest acknowledgment that long-form writing is a real form of creative expression and deserves a proper home of its own.

This very book will most likely be the first thing offered through Creative Zone, a field report from someone with no coding background who managed to build a platform with the help of AI. Other writers are just as welcome to feature their books on Kora. Artists can set up gallery-style presentations of their work. Comic creators can run ongoing series. All of that is possible right here.

At the moment, this zone is still close to a blank sheet of paper. I hope artists, writers, and other creators will share ideas and help shape it into something that actually serves their needs.

General social content, meaning everyday videos, photos, discussion, news, and ordinary posting, belongs in the Local, National, and Global Zones, where it can find the right audience by geography and topic instead of having to compete against dedicated creative work on terms that were never meant for it.

Collective Direction

This is the zone that makes KoraUS fundamentally different from every other platform out there.

Collective Direction is KoraUS's attempt to bring direct public participation online, at real scale, in a form that fits the way we live now.

The basic idea is simple: any user can post an issue in the Collective Direction zone, be it a civic problem, a policy question, a public concern, or anything else that genuinely invites a real public response. Other users can then weigh in with their own positions. They can support it, oppose it, refine it, or push back on it. Over time, the platform is meant to reveal where the participating public actually stands. Not where the loudest voices land, and not where the most viral framing points, but what the real spread of opinion looks like among the people who have chosen to take part.

Once discussion on a given issue slows down enough, the open discussion phase can close. The positions that drew enough support to make the cutoff can then move into a refinement phase, where additional debate can further clarify each position.

What comes out the other end is meant to be more than a poll and more than a petition. The goal is a structured, deliberative process, one that gives complicated issues enough room to actually breathe, keeps minority positions visible right alongside majority ones, and makes it possible to watch whether opinion shifts as more people join in and more information enters the conversation.

It is important to be honest about the limits here. KoraUS has no power to compel anyone to do anything at all. It cannot force politicians, corporations, or institutions to lift a finger. What it can do is map the public's position clearly, transparently, and in a form that becomes genuinely hard to ignore. Politicians who claim to speak for their constituents, companies that claim to answer to public demand, and communities trying to figure out what they themselves actually believe would all be able to look at that map. The platform never tells anyone what they must do. It simply makes it a good deal harder to pretend the public's position does not exist.

On KoraUS, political discussion is meant to be pointed back toward civic problems and possible solutions, away from partisan spectacle, away from team loyalty, and away from outrage performed for the benefit of an algorithm. If you want to talk politics here, the expectation is that you dig into what the problem actually is, who it affects, what the real options are, and what you think honestly should happen. The platform is built to steer everything else toward something more useful.

This is, I will freely admit, a belief. It is a belief that people, given the right structure around them, may take on hard questions more honestly than the current platforms have taught us to expect. Those platforms have spent years optimizing for the worst instincts in us. Collective Direction is an experiment in whether a different structure can coax out something better.

This part of Kora will eventually need AI to work properly.

Imagine ten people posting ten slightly different versions of what is really the same idea. Those should not be treated as ten entirely separate ideas forever. At scale, the platform needs a way to recognize when many users are expressing the same underlying position and to count that position accurately, in real time, as it happens. That is genuinely hard to do by hand, and it is hard to do well with traditional software on its own. AI can help here by mapping sentiment, grouping similar ideas together, and keeping the whole discussion legible even as participation keeps growing.

This does not call for a full, general-purpose AI system. What it calls for is something much narrower and far more carefully controlled: an AI agent designed specifically for this one task and audited closely along the way. With an AI Committee regularly checking samples and reviewing the outcomes, Kora could rely on a simpler, more transparent AI layer built to do exactly what the platform needs and nothing beyond that.

As things stand today, Kora runs no AI on the platform. In the beginning, Kora will run on leased infrastructure, the way most smaller applications do, and the hardware available there is limited. A fully working Collective Direction system, with live aggregation happening at meaningful scale, will almost certainly need stronger infrastructure than Kora has at launch. So this zone may well begin in a simpler form and grow into its full shape later, once the platform is large enough and the infrastructure sturdy enough to support dedicated AI agents.

Until that AI is in place, this whole process will be handled by hand as carefully and as well as it possibly can be.

Votes in Progress

Every Collective Direction discussion that makes it through the refinement phase can then move into a vote by the whole user base. The ideas that remain meaningfully competitive, based on how many users took part and how many distinct positions emerged, would be placed into a voting cycle that runs on a regular schedule. The current thinking is a weekly cycle running from Tuesday through the following Monday. Once a refinement phase wraps up, that issue simply waits its turn in the queue for the next cycle to come around.

People could step into this zone whenever they liked, sort the items by Local, National, or Global category, look over whatever is currently up for a vote, and cast their ballots at their own pace during the open cycle. In that sense, this zone is the formal decision layer of Collective Direction, the place where discussion finally stops being just discussion and becomes a measurable expression of where the public stands.

Mixed Discovery

This zone pulls together an aggregated feed drawn from the Local, National, and Global Zones all at once. When you do not have the time to visit each zone separately, or you simply are not in the mood to spend your evening in one particular corner of the platform, Mixed Discovery gives you an easier, more relaxed way to scroll along and catch what is happening across all the different places at a glance.

Kids Zone

This zone is not ready for display yet.

I have spent a lot of time thinking about making Kids Zone a distinct part of the platform, perhaps with separate spaces set aside for preschool, elementary, junior high, and high school age groups. As a parent of two teenagers myself, I know firsthand how genuinely hard it is to manage screen time for kids. Too much of it can take a toll on their psychology, their physical health, their posture, their social behavior, their moral development, and plenty more besides. And yet, at the same time, I can see that their online time is often just an extension of their offline relationships. Their school friendships keep going after the final bell through screens. They work through assignments together, plan birthday parties, and stay socially connected in ways that feel completely real to them.

That tension is exactly what makes this so difficult. It is far too simple to say that less screen time is always the right answer. Priorities certainly matter, but in real life, priorities and online activity often have a way of blurring together until they are hard to pull apart.

So I have chosen to leave this zone open for a broader conversation. Parents, educators, child-development experts, and young people themselves should all have a real voice in shaping what a space like this ought to become. Together we can work through what kind of online platform would actually serve different age groups well.

This is exactly the sort of question that Kora is built to work through out in the open.

ONE UPLOAD SURFACE FOR THREE UPLOAD ROUTES

Content enters KoraUS through the plus sign up in the top navigation bar, which opens a single upload surface that then branches into three separate paths. This is more than a small technical detail. It is a deliberate design choice, and there is a real philosophy sitting behind it.

The first route is for posts. These are the text-based contributions: questions, opinions, links to news, discussions, arguments, civic commentary. This is the short-form layer of the platform, built for quick response and back-and-forth debate. When you post something into a zone, it travels through this route and drops straight into that zone's ongoing conversation.

The second route is for content, and this is the media path. It handles videos and images presented in a clean, structured format, complete with a thumbnail, a tidy card layout, and proper rendering across the different parts of the platform. When someone uploads a video to the National Zone about a holiday trip, a memorable meal, or a policy issue, or shares a set of images in the Local Zone about some change in the neighborhood, it all flows through this route. The whole point is to let the platform handle the presentation cleanly, so you never have to stop and fuss over formatting every single time you want to share something.

The third route is for creative work. Books, essays, artwork, music, comics, films, and other projects that belong in the Creative Zone all travel this way. This route treats creative work as its own kind of system, with its own internal logic and its own presentation, instead of squeezing it into a post with a few extra fields tacked on or a piece of media wearing a different label.

So why three routes instead of one simple pipe?

Because every platform that pushes everything through a single, undifferentiated content pipeline eventually ends up rewarding whatever happens to perform best inside that pipeline. Short, provocative posts start to beat thoughtful essays. Quick reaction videos start to outrun more careful, considered work. The algorithm quietly learns what draws the strongest response and then serves up more and more of it, and over time the whole platform bends itself around that logic until everything looks the same.

Keeping the routes separate is the structural defense against exactly that kind of drift.

Each route is built to serve a different kind of expression, and that separation lets each kind of expression simply be what it is, judged by the standards that actually suit it, without being forced to compete against things that are fundamentally different in nature. A thoughtful thousand-word post about local water quality should never have to out-click a reaction video just to reach the people it was written for. A book should never have to compete against idle scrolling at all. The three routes are how KoraUS keeps these very different forms from collapsing into one flattened mush. In the end, it comes down to respecting the effort a creator put in by respecting the container that effort arrives in.

THE CHAT SYSTEM

Kora has two distinct chat systems, and it really helps to understand how the two differ in what they do and who they are for.

The Private Chat System

The regular chat system is private, plain and simple. You can reach it through the chat icon in the top navigation bar, and it is built for personal communication between users. It is never public-facing, and it is not a committee workspace. It is strictly the platform's private messaging utility, meant for your own conversations.

This system handles both one-to-one messages and group messaging. As Kora's user base grows, we plan to fold in voice and video calling and video conferencing so that people can stay connected in even richer ways.

CommitteeChat System

CommitteeChat exists for an entirely different reason. It lives exclusively inside committees, where it works as a public-facing tool for getting things done, letting committee members coordinate their tasks right out in full view of the community. It is a working part of Kora's governance and workflow, and it is deliberately not a channel for private user conversation.

Inside CommitteeChat, workgroups can sharpen their focus even further through work item sub-chats. This keeps even the most tangled, complicated projects organized, easy to navigate, and fully transparent to anyone watching.

Committee-wide and project-wide discussions run through the Public Announcement Chat system. Much like CommitteeChat, this system lets people spin up sub-chat groups so that smaller conversations can happen whenever they are needed, without cluttering the main thread.

WHERE IT STANDS

KoraUS is live right now at KoraUS.app on the web, iOS, and Android. As of this writing, it sits in beta, which means real users, real governance structures, and real committees, all waiting for volunteers to step in and bring them to life.

The foundation is built. The experiment is genuinely underway.

What comes next is a lot more than just software. Kora still needs refinement, more users, more volunteers, and plenty more public testing out in the open. It will need additional modules, smoother workflows, stronger committee participation, and, further down the road, country-specific deployments if the model proves itself useful beyond the United States.

This book is part of what comes next.

KoraUS is unusual enough that the platform really did need to be explained on its own terms, which is much of what this chapter has tried to do. But the book is also a field report on what it means to build with large language models: how the platform actually came together, what went wrong along the way, what went right, and what it genuinely feels like to collaborate with AI on something this large and this real.

The people who read this book and then join the platform may well turn out to be the very people who help shape what KoraUS becomes. That connection between the book and the platform is completely intentional, and I am counting on it.

In the end, KoraUS will only succeed if enough people come to believe it is worth building together. It was built for its users from the start, and it is meant to be owned and run by them.

EPILOGUE

Kora was built to be a tool, not a media channel or an attention machine.

A tool for helping people separate evidence from noise. A tool for mapping majority consensus. A tool that lets people own and manage their own data. A place where anyone with a story can tell it. A place to express your life, engage your community, and debate the civic issues that actually affect you.

The data industry has grown enormous over the past two decades, and it will only keep growing. Corporations are already competing hard for market share in it. In the process, the public risks becoming more divided, more surveilled, and more exploited than it already is.

We can stop that.

The public can own its own data. It can use the financial value of that data for public purposes rather than corporate profit. A platform owned and operated by its users is not a utopian idea. It is an engineering problem. And we now have a starting point.

Kora itself came out of the same lesson this book has been circling from the beginning: powerful tools do not govern themselves. AI did not build Kora by itself, and Kora will not govern itself. Both require people willing to manage power, limits, rules, and consequences.

It may seem foolhardy and daunting until enough people decide it is worth trying.

What happens next is up to the people on it.

This is not a finished product handed to you.

It is an unfinished platform handed to all of us.

www.ingramcontent.com/pod-product-compliance
Lightning Source LLC
LaVergne TN
LVHW022155200926
848481LV00006B/1750